Food as Foreplay

Recipes for Romance, Love and Lust

The Cooking Couple

Illustrations by Michael Miracle

ALEXANDRIA PRESS
Cambridge, MA 02140

Food As Foreplay Copyright © 1996 by Ellen and Michael Albertson.

All rights reserved.

"The Cooking Couple™" is a trademark of Ellen and Michael Albertson denoting a series of books, other publications and products relating to cooking.

First Printing
Printed and bound in the United States of America.
10 9 8 7 6 5 4 3 2

Published by:
Alexandria Press™
P.O. Box 987
Cambridge Massachusetts 02140

Publisher's Cataloging in Publication Data
Albertson, Ellen R. 1962
Albertson, Michael L. 1956
Includes Index
1. Cooking 2. Self-help 3. Relationships 4. How-to 5. Title
ISBN 0-9646649-0-9

Library of Congress Catalog Card Number
95-078452

Bookstore Distribution: Login Publishers Consortium

Attention: Quantity discounts are available on bulk purchases of this book. Excerpts, special books or articles can also be created for specific needs. For information, please contact Alexandria Press, Special Editions, P.O. Box 987, Cambridge, MA 02140, or call (617) 641-1838 / fax (617) 646-5194.

Illustrations © Michael Miracle
Text design by Joyce C. Weston
Cover design by Joyce C. Weston, Tony deFigio, and Eric Bertelsen
Photography by Lynn McCann

This book is dedicated to our parents for teaching us
how to cook, thrive, and survive.

Special thanks to:
Paula Derrow for her sharp pencil and sharper wit.
Lynn McCann for her patience and artistry.
Faun Fitter for her help in making the book better.
Ken Lehrhoff and Jay Fedigan of Powerglide Media for their
humor, support, advise and invaluable insights into the
demented workings of the artistic mind.

and to:

Gregory J. P. Godek for blazing the trail and showing us the way.
Thank you, Greg.

CONTENTS

PREFACE

Heat up Your Love Life

"One cannot think well, love well, sleep well,
if one has not dined well."

— *Virginia Woolf*

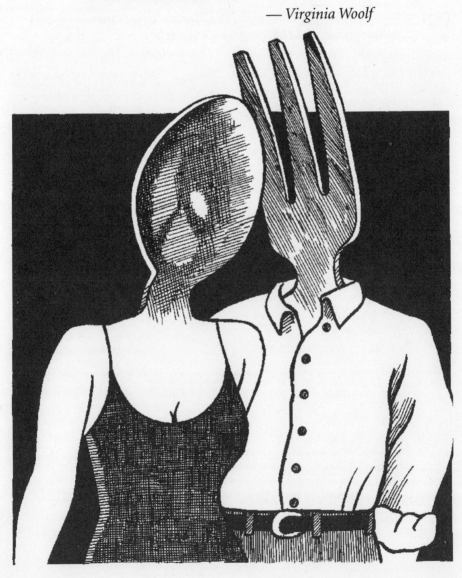

*I*f the sizzle in your relationship has started to fizzle or you're looking for a new playmate to grease the gears of love, pull out the frying pan and heat up your love life. Cupid estimates that two out of three couples do not meet the Recommended Daily Allowance for romance. Meals provide three opportunities a day to increase your RDAs and unleash passion. Make time to enjoy and prepare meals together — investing in time, bread and wine pays off in romance.

Food, sex and romance have been linked for centuries. It's no coincidence that in America, where home-cooked meals are often an afterthought, we have the highest divorce rate (about 50%) of any developed country. In France, where the divorce rate is one-fifth of America's, fast food is a national disaster and romance a way of life. The French value and cultivate a passion for food. In France even the ingredients are sexy. Take "pomme d'amour," French for "love-apple." To us stodgy Americans, it's a tomato. In France, every meal is an occasion to celebrate sensuality and toast love, romance and life. Good food served on a bed of romance leads to a happy, healthy, long, loving life together.

Go open a bottle of bordeaux and toast your love! Don't wait for a special occasion or the weekend. Dine in tonight, unless you miss big bills, long lines and obnoxious waiters who forget your appetizer, but always remember to put it on your check. For the price of a meal at a moderate restaurant, you can enjoy an extraordinary meal with wine and dessert in the privacy of your home. Plus, you don't have to leave a tip. Share a simple plate of figs, prosciutto and shrimp. Dress up for dinner. Play dreamy music and take a spin around the living room. You may not be Fred and Ginger, but we bet your partner gives you straight tens and kisses for dessert.

Ever watch a couple eat? You can determine a lot about their relationship from how they interact over the table. Do they share food? When she dips into

---

THE MAGIC OF FOOD

If you don't believe food can enchant, rent *Like Water for Chocolate* and watch as the heroine, Tita, woos her lover, Pedro, with Quail in Rose Petal Sauce.

Food can feed faith and lift spirits. In the Bible, Jesus transformed five loaves and two fishes into a meal for spiritually and physically starved multitudes.

Food can usher in a happy or prosperous year. During Chinese New Year you may be served coin-shaped dumplings to bring wealth. Visit a Jewish home on Rosh Hashanah (Jewish New Year), and you'll dip apples in honey for a sweet year.

his gravy, does he scowl or smile? Does she feed him bites of brownie? Or do they remain at opposite ends of the table exchanging only crumbs of conversation? Sharing food is a sign of intimacy. Reaching across the table and taking a bite of your date's dinner shows you are comfortable with each other. Would you do this at a business lunch? Of course not.

Human beings have always shared food for rituals, ceremonies, holidays and feasts. What would Thanksgiving be without family, turkey and bursting bellies? How could we celebrate Halloween without candy, a birthday without cake or the Fourth of July without barbecue? Food is a social, religious, artistic and political statement. Think about where Marie Antoinette's famous line "Let them eat cake" got her.

Food is crucial for survival and a delight to the senses, yet food is much more than a source of nourishment and pleasure. It sustains life and embodies the earth's energy, which in turn, fills us with passion. Food can enchant your lover, feed faith or cure illness. Food helped you evolve from a baby into an adult and remains a magical tool to transform your body, your soul and the one you love. Food is a love letter that helps couples understand each other and grow closer.

Every meal is a chance to cherish your mate and express your sensuality. Food awakens the senses, puts us in the mood and enhances the moment. Food is sensuous, suggestive, playful and sexy. Don't be afraid to have fun with food. That's the whole point, having fun with food, your lover and life.

Remember, an aphrodisiac isn't some secret ingredient you buy from a gnarled old women who lives in a tree. It is the resonance, tone, timbre that YOU bring to cooking. Love radiates from your heart, seeps into the food and gives it the mystical quality that ignites the soul. The real aphrodisiac is you.

The kitchen, like the bedroom, is a great place to have fun, woo each other and define boundaries. Who makes the first move? Who cooks, who shops, who stirs? Are you comfortable working together? How do you feel when she tastes your soup and suggests adding pepper? Does your relationship hinge on perfect sex or creating the perfect meal, or do you both laugh and eat scrambled eggs when the soufflé falls? Remember, mutuality is the key component in any relationship. Share chores, bills and responsibilities, and there will be enough good times to go around for everyone.

APHRODISIACS

Many foods have developed a reputation as aphrodisiacs over the centuries. Eggs (caviar), foods with phallic shapes (bananas, carrots, cucumbers and asparagus) or those resembling female genitals (oysters, figs) were often thought to evoke desire.

WHEN IN ROME

Do you think it was an accident that Roman emperors did their own cooking or entrusted a family member with the responsibility? Too bad in Augustus's case this proved to be a fatal mistake. His wife Livia, known for her dignified beauty, her chastity and pleasant personality, was also known for her skill at mixing poisons and other less lethal potions.

"I think just a little more hemlock and a pinch of salt would taste just about right. Augustus dear… dinner's ready."

At least Livia was an equal opportunity chef. It's believed that she hastened the demise of Augustus's nephew Marcellus in 23 B.C., Lucius and Gaius (Marcellus's grandsons), as well as dear Augustus, with her culinary creations. Gives a whole new meaning to the phrase "too spicy."

Most recipes in this book are designed to cook together. You can grate the cheese while your lover slices salmon and kisses your neck. Cooking healthy meals is the best way to show your love and take care of each other. When you cook for someone, you nurture them physically and spiritually. They in turn trust you with their life, literally.

So, surprise and enchant your date with a gourmet meal after gourmet lovemaking. Many of our recipes can be prepared in advance or held in the oven for hours so you can focus on each other instead of worrying about the quiche. Hey, let's be honest, the food can wait.

When you break from lovemaking, a wonderful feast awaits. Believe us: Postcoitus food tastes best. Don't have the time or inclination to prepare dinner? Just don't feel like cooking? This book contains easy recipes, like Impromptu Fondue, that can be whipped up at the last minute. We suggest The Cooking Couple Grazing Tray, in Chapter 12, a delicious array of nibbles to be laid out and eaten throughout the evening.

TABLE FOR TWO

This book is about cooking for yourself and the one you love and/or lust after, so all our recipes are designed for two. Whether you consume the entire recipe in a postcoitus frenzy or leave leftovers for a midnight snack or picnic is up to you. Our servings are generous to accommodate The Cooking Couple's golden rule: Always make plenty and always have goodies waiting in the pantry in case dinner burns.

Cooking is food alchemy. A handful of this, a pinch of that and violà: A killer creation or soul-satisfying masterpiece emerges from the cauldron. As you stockpile recipes and ingredients, cooking becomes intuitive and creative. You'll wonder why you didn't start sooner. All the recipes in our book (okay... most of them; sometimes we show off) are quick, easy, seductive and fun. Be flexible, leave time to enjoy meals and your mate. Cooking should be an adventure not a chore. Forget making perfect hollandaise sauce. Enjoy the experience and live in the moment. If dinner burns, open a bottle of champagne, toast your future, nibble your lover's neck and order take-out.

These recipes are a means to an end, not an end in themselves. Like sex, cooking is about learning, experimenting and experiencing. Discover which foods turn the two of you on and savor them together. One couple may be aroused by meatloaf and mashed potatoes. Another may find sesame noodles sexy.

Remember the foods that chaperoned your courtship? We fell in love over nachos. Try childhood favorites and turn it into a game. Macaroni and cheese, Oreos, ice cream sandwiches, Twinkies. Experiment with new foods. Have you ever sampled fried alligator tail? Wear that slinky red dress and the spikes that make your legs look like they go from here to there and back again, and Spam will taste like caviar.

The key is mood and attitude.

1

Out of Eden and Into the Fire

"Cooking is like love. It should be entered into with abandon or not at all."

— *Harriet Van Horne*

*I*n the beginning, God created heaven and earth, the fish of the sea, the birds of the sky and all living things that creep on the earth. Finally, God made Adam and Eve and blessed them: "Be fertile and multiply, fill the earth and master it." God gave them a no-money-down, 0% mortgage on a cushy split level in Eden. Then the trouble started. One day Eve was hanging out, minding her own business when the serpent, the shrewdest of all the wild beasts and a neighbor who can really ruin your property value, convinced her to eat the forbidden fruit. She took a bite and gave Adam a taste. The pair were expelled from the garden and life hasn't been the same since. No more running around in the buff, no more free lunch and no more painless childbirth.

Humankind has come a long way since forbidden fruit and the first loincloth. The origins of the first chef remain a mystery. Our primitive ancestors probably developed a hunger for cooked food, which tasted better and was easier to chew and digest, after eating animals caught in a fire. The next step in cookery came when humans tamed fire. According to Greek legend, Prometheus stole fire from the gods and was tortured by Zeus for the crime.

Grilled or roasted food first appeared after the great Ice Age, about 12,000 years ago. Later, people learned to cook with hot stones. For pots and pans our ancestors used holes in the ground, animal skins, skulls and eventually pottery. Cooking wasn't fun and it certainly wasn't romantic.

Today, technology builds our fires. Stoves, grills, ovens and microwaves make cooking a pleasure and a romantic playground. Equip your kitchen with a large skillet or wok, a smaller sauté pan a stockpot, a saucepan, a couple sharp knives, a vegetable peeler, a cutting board and a food processor or blender, and you'll be cooking in no time.

COOKING IS A LEARNING PROCESS

The more you cook the better you will become, and the greater culinary risks you will be able and willing to take. Start out with a cheese omelette and work your way up to a soufflé. Grill a piece of swordfish and serve with a lemon wedge. Notice how the fish tastes. The next time you make swordfish, rub the fish with olive oil and coriander, grill and serve with a few different salsas. (Try our mango, kiwi, pineapple.) Sound judgment and frequent sampling will determine what works for you.

LOW-FAT AND LUSCIOUS

All of our recipes are designed with lovers in mind. So, they're decadent, delicious and oh yes, sometimes fattening. If you're watching your weight or cholesterol level, curtail dessert and look for recipes that don't lean heavily on butter or oil.

You can also substitute low-fat products for full-fat ingredients. Here are some suggestions to help you cut the fat.

- Use skim or 1% milk instead of whole or 2%.
- Replace each egg yolk with 1 egg white or 1/8 cup egg substitute.
- Substitute yogurt for sour cream.
- Use low-fat cheese instead of regular.
- Try leaner meats (extra-lean or 95% lean).
- Substitute ground turkey or extra-lean beef for regular ground beef.
- Bake, broil, boil, roast, grill or steam foods.
- Eat more beans and grains and less meat.
- Use cooking spray to grease pans instead of oil.
- Cook with wine, broth and tomato sauce instead of frying or sautéing.

Whether you're a gourmet cook, with a Martha Stewart deluxe kitchen and a matching apron and hair tie or infamous for your scorched grilled cheese à la mode, here are some general guidelines for amorous gastronomic success.

1. Prepare and eat foods you like. Don't serve escargot to impress your date if you think cooked snails resemble rubber hot dogs with their tongues hanging out.

2. Make meals special even if you're just mastering spaghetti. Set time aside to plan, prepare and enjoy food. Remember, candles, wine and a smile turn Ragu into amore.

3. Create balance nutritionally. Eat well, but not too well, and your body will reward you with energy and vitality. Care for your body and it will run better and be more fun to drive whether you're taking a spin around the block or around the boudoir. Stuffing yourself occasionally is fine, but eating should not be a daily free-for-all.

All of our recipes are delicious and many are low in fat. Some, we admit, could get Ellen excommunicated from the American Dietetic Association. But the occasional indulgence, especially after 45 minutes on the Stairmaster at level eight, is fine, fun and healthy. So loosen up. Your waistline can handle an occasional slice of double deep, double dark, double rich, double chocolate pudding cake.

4. Create balance aesthetically. To keep dinner interesting and your partner interested, nix monotone meals. Toddlers eat yellow pasta, yellow squash, yellow cheese and apple sauce. You're a grownup now. Mix flavors and colors. Don't serve coconut rice with coconut curry and coconut cream pie. Flex your textures. Cauliflower, mashed potatoes and boiled cod are nutritionally sound, but blah. Mushy dinners that resemble spackling compound aren't sexy. Substitute broccoli for cauliflower, crispy potatoes for mashed and salmon for cod. Now you've got a plate. Think of cooking as art and paint your partner's palate. Color and contrast transform the mundane into a marvel.

5. Experiment with your tastes. (You had to learn how to kiss, remember?) With a little practice and exploration you'll enter a private world of culinary delights and tantalizing nights.

6. Improvise recipes. Subscribe to a cooking magazine. Watch a cooking show. Buy a new cut of meat, fish or poultry, and add an exotic spice or interesting sauce. Throw macadamia nuts into the brownies instead of walnuts. Stop at a farm stand for fresh chervil or blackberries.

7. Don't go overboard. Use common sense when you experiment and keep meals simple. Fresh fruit is the perfect foil for roast duck; an ice cream bomb isn't.

8. Let food enliven all your senses. Taste, smell, texture, color and temperature work together to create a chorus of flavor. Before eating we see, smell and touch food. The tiny receptors on the tongue, called papillae, only sense sweet, salty, bitter and sour. The eating experience involves all the senses. Let them work together.

ANTHRISCUS CEREFOLIUM

Chervil, parsley's frilly cousin, resembles the poisonous hemlock. Don't worry, it's harmless and may have medicinal value as a weight loss aid.

In the Middle Ages men wounded in battle were given chervil juice to help determine who would live. Those who could stomach the plant were given a better chance of survival.

You don't need to be wounded to enjoy this delicate herb. Chervil is a key ingredient in béarnaise sauce and makes a pretty garnish. Toss it in omelettes, chicken dishes or salads. Just be sure to use fresh chervil. The dried variety has very little flavor.

SEXY SMELLS

You probably know that certain smells are a turn on. But did you know that the smell of some foods actually increases blood flow to the penis?

The Smell and Taste Treatment and Research Foundation in Chicago discovered that homey kitchen smells, like cinnamon buns and pumpkin pie, may be more powerful than Chanel N°5.

In one study, 31 men had their penile blood flow measured while inhaling 46 different odors including doughnut, roasting meat, baby powder, peppermint, cheese pizza, buttered popcorn, lilly of the valley, green apple, cranberry, chocolate and orange.

According to the study, a mixture of lavender and pumpkin pie; doughnut and black licorice; and pumpkin pie and doughnut all significantly increased penile blood flow.

Strawberry aroused men who felt sexually satisfied. Older men responded best to vanilla. Men who reported that they had sex frequently were particularly stimulated by cola, oriental spice and lavender.

Approximately a thousand receptors in the nasal cavity make it possible to perceive a multitude of smells. The aroma of baking bread, simmering soup or grilling meat lures you into the kitchen long before dinner is ready. Our primitive sense of smell has the power to spark memories and emotions and even helps determine whom we chose as a mate.

The sight of food, like its smell, can also make you salivate and run to the kitchen or grocery store. That's why watching T.V., with its glut of food commercials, makes you hungry. Color, shape and texture all play a role. Imagine how plump, ripe, red strawberries dipped into a cool cloud of smooth, sweet cream or a warm pool of silky chocolate taste. What about a wonderfully decadent, dreamy, delectable cheesecake prominently displayed in a bakery window. Salivating yet? It's time to engage your mouth. Take a bite. Let taste flow across your tongue and enjoy the sensory experience of eating.

9. Food, like sex, should be natural. Buy the freshest, best quality ingredients you can, and enhance their flavor with the special charm that only you can bring to your lover's plate. Avoid artificial flavors and colors and foods with labels that read like the formula for Windex.

HERE COME THE BRIDE & GROOM
WITH THEIR FORKS & SPOONS

OK, since you asked, our wedding menu was...

Appetizers
Buffalo Chicken Wings
Duck in Wanton Skins
Taco Station with Eight Salsas
Barbecued Shrimp

Entrees
Grilled Lobster Tails
Pesto Stuffed Chicken Breasts

Side Dishes
Fried Yellow, Green and Cherry
  Tomatoes

Wild Mushroom Salad with Wild
  Rice
Challah
Focaccia

Dessert
Blueberry Pie (now a Cooking
  Couple anniversary tradition)
Chocolate Torte
Rain Forest Crunch Ice Cream
Passion Fruit Sorbet
Raspberry Basil Sorbet

And we *never* fought about it.
Michael let Ellen pick everything.

---

10. **Have fun and prepare meals together.** There'll be no resentment about who has to do the work and plenty of fanny patting opportunities. You don't want to feel that you are always the one in the kitchen, do you? So open the wine, turn up the stereo, sing along and chop to the beat. You'll also learn a lot about your mate. Is your kitchen cramped or does he/she cramp your style? Better to find out now than when arguing about what to serve at the wedding.

11. **When they ask if it's your recipe, answer with a smile and a kiss.** If they ask again, keep kissing. Continue until they shut up and kiss back.

12. **Leave the dishes.** Nothing breaks the mood of a great meal more than playing busboy at the end of the adventure. Head straight upstairs and leave the mess for the morning. For The Cooking Couple, cleanup means showering together.

13. **Get out of the kitchen and into the bedroom.** This book is about eating and fun, NOT kitchen prison. There are no desserts because you are dessert. Of course you may become the first course, in which case let food cap your lovemaking like an after-dinner cordial that renews your vigor for a late-night snack. Don't light a cigarette. Light your appetite with our sexy, romantic, fun-loving, great-tasting dishes. It's time to let down your hair, roll up your sleeves, pour the wine, turn on the music and get cookin'.

CHICKEN TUSCANY

A side of pasta or rice, steamed asparagus or a salad and a glass of white bordeaux turn this dish into an elegant meal.

2 large red peppers
2 boneless, skinless chicken breast halves
1 teaspoon olive oil
Salt and freshly ground black pepper, to taste
½ cup fresh spinach, chopped
5 ounces mozzarella cheese, grated

1. Preheat broiler.
2. Cut tops off the red peppers and remove seeds and membrane. Roast peppers by placing under the broiler briefly and turning several times until skin is slightly singed. Remove peppers from the oven and let cool.
3. Lay the chicken flat between two sheets of wax paper. Using the side of a mallet or cleaver, pound chicken until it's about ¼-inch thick. Moisten each breast with ½ teaspoon olive oil and sprinkle with salt and pepper. Cover each breast with ¼ cup chopped spinach and ½ cup mozzarella cheese. Tightly roll up chicken breasts and place in roasted peppers. Place in a baking dish. (Chicken can be prepared up to this point several hours in advance and kept in the refrigerator until you are ready to start dinner.)

4. Cook at 350°F for 45–50 minutes. Take peppers out. Place 2 additional tablespoons cheese on top of each pepper. Place under the broiler and cook until cheese is melted, about 5 minutes.

Variation: Use a slice of provolone and a slice of prosciutto instead of the mozzarella and spinach. Top with additional provolone before placing under the broiler.

NUTTY PASTA

Experiment with different types of pasta. We like this with rigatoni or penne.

½ pound pasta
2 tablespoons olive oil
2 medium garlic cloves, minced
½ cup Italian bread crumbs
¼ cup pine nuts
¼ cup Parmesan cheese, grated
Salt and freshly ground pepper, to taste

1. Boil salted water in a large pot. Add pasta and cook until pasta is al dente (firm yet tender).
2. Heat the olive oil in a large sauté pan over medium heat.
3. Add the garlic and sauté for 30 seconds.
4. Add the bread crumbs and pine nuts. Allow them to toast, stirring frequently until golden brown. If pasta isn't ready yet, set sauté pan aside.
5. Drain pasta. In a large serving bowl toss cooked pasta with the pine nut and bread crumb mixture, Parmesan cheese, salt and pepper.

CRAB BURRITOS WITH PEPPER SALAD

This Southwestern-inspired dish may seem difficult, but if you make the salad ahead of time preparation isn't much harder than opening a beer. We suggest Corona with a slice of lime.

PEPPER SALAD

1 red bell pepper
1 green bell pepper
1 cup summer squash, about ⅓ pound
2 tablespoons olive oil
2 tablespoons lime juice
2 tablespoons lemon juice
2 tablespoons fresh cilantro, minced
Salt and freshly ground black pepper, to taste

1. Cut the peppers in half, remove seeds and membrane and cut into

julienne strips. Cut the squash into julienne strips and place in a bowl with the peppers.

2. In a small bowl, combine the olive oil, lime juice, lemon juice and cilantro. Pour over the peppers and squash. Toss well. Add salt and pepper to taste. Refrigerate until ready to serve.

CRAB BURRITOS

> 6 flour tortillas
> 1 tablespoon vegetable oil
> 12 ounces surumi (imitation crab meat), diced
> 8 ounces jalapeno jack cheese, grated
> 1 cup fresh tomato, chopped, about 2 medium-size tomatoes
> ¾ cup prepared salsa
> ⅓ cup sour cream

1. Preheat oven to 325°F. Wrap the flour tortillas in aluminum foil and place in oven until heated through, about 10–15 minutes.

2. Heat the oil in a medium-size saucepan over medium heat. Add the surumi and cook until heated through, about 2–3 minutes. Add cheese and tomato and cook until cheese is melted.

3. Lay a tortilla flat. Place several spoonfuls of crab mixture in center of tortilla. Roll tortilla around filling. Repeat for remaining tortillas.

4. To serve, place two filled tortillas, seam side down, in center of a plate. Place a spoonful of Pepper Salad to one side and a spoonful of salsa topped with a dab of sour cream on the other.

Passion-Filled Pantry

"The music I heard with you was more than music. And the bread I broke with you was more than bread."

— *Conrad Aiken*

*C*onvincing your dining companion that you're a great cook is easy if you own the complete works of Julia Child, don't have a job or children and have all day to shop, cook and discuss recipes with Mom. But that ain't us and it sure ain't you. Like the rest of the world, you probably work 50 hours a week, have little time to buy and prepare food and don't always feel like talking to Mom.

What happens when you need to whip up a wonderful meal on a moment's notice? Does a jet of fear run up your spine? Feel whipped even before you plug in the mixer? Does your refrigerator contain only a stale loaf of Wonder Bread and a pound of ground round that's about to walk to the garbage on its own? That's fine for an evening with Seinfeld but not for your date. If you don't pull off a miracle, your date will be headed back to the redhead in accounting, and your cooking reputation will be in the trash faster than that ground beef.

To stoke Saturday night romance you need a well-stocked pantry. No room? Nonsense. Grab a box and store staples under your bed. Don't be embarrassed. Your date will probably find your sprint to the bedroom for ingredients endearing. In fact, your guest might follow you and forget about dinner.

Fast and easy, that's how cooking will be with a well-stocked pantry. Stocking up on chicken broth, quick-cooking rice mixes, pasta and canned beans will transform impotent leftovers into an erotic feast. Stores are filled with high-quality packaged and prepared foods that minimize prep time and make meals wonderful. A few fresh ingredients plus a drop of secret sauce will send your dinner and date over the top. And they'll think you did it all from scratch.

VANILLA OR CHOCOLATE? YOUR PLACE OR MINE?

Ask a question about something in their cart. That's how we met. It was a Sunday afternoon in June. Ellen was procrastinating over low-fat, no-fat, sugar-free and light frozen yogurts. Michael was reaching for a half gallon of cookies and cream (the flavor that Ellen was secretly lusting over).

"Is that stuff any good?" Michael asked.

"Not really, but it's got a lot less fat and calories than what you're buying," Ellen said.

"You don't look like you have to worry about calories," Michael said. "Why don't you come over to my place for a scoop and indulge?"

Flattered, Ellen accepted and the rest is history — a lifelong love affair built on a bowl of cookies and cream.

A BRIEF HISTORY OF FRENCH FRIES AND FRENCH KISSES

The French gave us champagne, the French bulldog, French bread, French windows, French dressing and the French horn; but the French can't take credit for that fast food favorite: the French fry. Our ancestors (good old potato loving, vodka swigging Russian immigrants) probably invented the first French fry on the boardwalk of Coney Island, New York, around the turn of the century. The deep-fried strips of potato were given the name "French" fry because of the way they were cut, called "frenched" (in thin strips).

The French also take credit for French kisses. This is false. After much research, we have discovered that French kisses were actually invented in Peoria, Iowa, in 1922 by Johnson Medson, an unemployed laborer, and his cow Betsy.

Still not convinced? Still single? Pick up a mate with that pound of steak. Don't just shop for bananas. Check out the tasty homosapiens in the frozen-food aisle. Start a conversation with a potential dinner mate while selecting soup. You can discover a lot about people from their grocery carts. Stouffer's Salisbury steak and chocolate cake, this shopper's probably short on time and on the way to a big waistline. Balsamic vinegar, sun-dried tomatoes and cilantro, definitely a foodie. This gourmet probably cooks by candlelight and makes love in the afternoon with the windows open. Who do you want cooking for you? Who do you want kissing you?

> "I love these philosophical questions, Ellen."
> "Think less and write more, Sophocles. Remember, no dinner till this chapter is done."
> "Thy spoon is silver, thy wit is bitter; I shall write quick 'cause I want my dinner."

Follow the hunk or hunkette you've been eying into the ice cream section. Ask, "What's your favorite flavor?" Buy a pint on the spot and invite him/her over for a scoop. Stop going to superficial singles bars, getting drunk and ditching nerds with pocket protectors who want your Internet number. The supermarket is a natural. Imagine telling your grandchildren that you met in the pickle aisle and fell in love over produce.

Convinced? Grab a cart and let's go shopping. The foods we suggest are available at most supermarkets. For variety check out gourmet or ethnic markets. Be adventurous. Visit an Asian or Arabic market where no one speaks English and all the jars are covered with hieroglyphics. Your date will be impressed even if your mystery food is stewed kashkan testicles in tomato sauce.

We'll start in the produce section with good old potatoes. Spuds are a cheap staple that can be mashed, boiled, baked, fried, roasted, microwaved, sautéed, scalloped, sliced, diced and served with everything from steak to green eggs and ham. If you have potatoes and oil, you've got America's favorite fast food, French fries. Buy spuds that are rock-hard, store in a cool, dark, dry place, and they'll keep for several weeks. When they grow more testicles than the stewed kashkan, it's time to toss 'em.

Don't forget onions. They can be fried, roasted, grilled or turned into French onion soup. Select good-sized, firm orbs (soft spots are nice on your partner, not on onions) and store in a cool, dark place away from the potatoes. Spuds and onions get along well in the pan, not the pantry. Throw a bag of carrots into the shopping cart as well. They'll keep for several weeks in the refrigerator and can be used in salads, as a side dish and in soups, stews and even muffins.

Ready for canned goods? Chicken stock is a must for sauces and soups. Always keep at least one jar of good-quality tomato sauce and a can of stewed or ground tomatoes on hand. You'll need two cans of clams, clam juice, evaporated milk, albacore tuna and several cans of beans. Kidney, cannellini, chickpeas and black beans will do. Don't like beans? You haven't tried them Cooking Couple style.

For the punch of flavor, color and texture that turns dishes from ordinary

---

STOP YOUR SOBBING

When raw onions are cut a sulfur compound is converted into an eye-irritating substance, called propenylsulfenic acid, which makes some people cry. Cold air or water slows down the process, helping to neutralize the chemical reaction and the tears.

If chopping onions makes you cry, try chilling peeled onions in cold water or in the refrigerator before cutting. This will slow down the tears and speed up the slicing. Michael sticks his whole head in the freezer and breathes through his nose when chopping onions and swears that it stops the tears.

to extraordinary stock up on roasted red peppers, capers (you don't know what capers are — trust us, buy them), garlic, artichoke hearts, black olives, good quality olive oil, vinegar (White and red wine vinegar are fine.), soy sauce and anchovies or anchovy paste. Other pantry basics include chocolate chips, corn starch, Tabasco sauce, flour, sugar and bread crumbs. Yes, this is a lot of food. But when you need to impress at a moment's notice, you'll be happy that your passion-filled pantry is full.

Oops, don't forget pasta. We're addicted to pasta, so we usually stock the equivalent of a case in assorted shapes, colors, textures and flavors. Sugar, fat and sodium free, pasta is the ultimate low-cost, carbo-loading chow. In Boston, marathoners eat it by the pound to get over Heart Break Hill. We're not sure if it will get you over your heartbreak, but make it right for that special somebody and you may never have to face heartbreak again. Personally we like ours with lots of garlic. But then again, we like most food with lots of garlic.

Add rice to your shopping list. Be adventurous. Try brown, basmati, wild or jasmine. We almost forgot ketchup (essential for fries). Salsa and chips are optional everywhere except at our house. Keeping crackers on hand is a smart move for spreadable foods (peanut butter, dips and gooey cheeses) and soups. We're never without Jiffy Corn Muffin Mix, the greatest invention since the dishwasher and at four boxes for a buck in most stores, "Oy, what a deal." Keep a bottle of vermouth in your pantry to use for Italian dishes calling for wine and a bottle of sherry for Asian dishes requiring wine.

Stash a loaf of French bread in the freezer to serve with meals and to use for dips and crostini. (What are crostini? Don't worry, we'll tell you later.) Frozen vegetables, nuts (we keep pine nuts, almonds, peanuts and walnuts on hand) and boneless chicken breasts (great for stir-frying and grilling) are other good items to keep in the freezer.

In the refrigerator keep mustard (we like Dijon and champagne), Parmesan cheese and another cheese such as cheddar or mozzarella, milk, butter, lemons, mayonnaise and eggs. Last, but not least, is a chilled bottle of champagne to make any meal special. Korbel for everyday use, Moët White Star for special occasions and Dom Perignon for very special occasions.

Okay, so what can you do with all these items? Don't worry, recipes follow.

SIX SUPER SUPPER STARTERS

1. Red Pepper Canapés Mix ½ cup roasted red peppers, cut in strips, with 1 tablespoon capers. Spread crackers or melba toast with a little cream cheese and top with the pepper mixture.

2. Nacho Platter Place a few handfuls of tortilla chips in the bottom of a large casserole dish. Sprinkle with ½ cup cheese (Monterey Jack, mozzarella and/or cheddar), ¼ cup salsa and 2 tablespoon each chopped onions, chopped jalapeno peppers and sliced olives. Continue to layer ingredients until you've used an entire (7–10 ounce) bag of chips. Bake at 350°F until cheese is melted and chips start to brown, about 15 minutes.

3. Hot Artichoke Dip In a blender or food processor, purée 1 (14 ounce) can drained artichoke hearts with 1 cup grated Parmesan cheese, ½ cup mayonnaise, 1 garlic clove and 1 tablespoon lemon juice. Place in a small crock or casserole dish. Top with another tablespoon Parmesan cheese, and bake at 350°F until bubbly and golden brown, about 20 minutes. Serve with pita bread, toasted French bread or cut-up vegetables.

4. Minestrone Soup Sauté 1 large, chopped onion in 1 tablespoon olive oil. Add 1 chopped carrot. Mix in 3 (16 ounce) cans chicken broth, 1 (16 ounce) can chopped tomatoes and 1 (16 ounce) can kidney beans. When the soup starts to boil reduce heat to simmer, add ½ cup pasta and let it cook in the soup until tender, about 10–15 minutes depending on the type of pasta. Finish with salt, pepper and 1–2 teaspoons dried Italian herbs.

5. Black Bean Soup In a large soup pot, sauté 1 large, finely chopped onion in 2 tablespoons vegetable oil. Add 3 minced garlic cloves, 1 tablespoon ground cumin, 1 teaspoon chili powder and ½ teaspoon crushed red pepper flakes. Sauté for 1–2 minutes, and take off the heat. Using a blender or food processor, purée 2 (16 ounce) cans undrained black beans with 1½ cups chicken broth and place in pot with the sautéed onion and spices. Add another can black beans and 1 teaspoon dried thyme. Simmer for about 20 minutes. Add salt and pepper to taste. Serve topped with yogurt or sour cream and scallions or cilantro and a side of taco chips for dipping.

CARROTS OVER EASY

For a simple, elegant side dish, sauté 4 sliced carrots in about 1 tablespoon butter, add 2 tablespoons orange juice and 1 tablespoon honey. Stir and serve.

PERFECT PASTA

To prevent water from boiling over (which will not impress your date), always cook pasta in a pot that holds at least two quarts water per half pound of pasta. Add about 1 teaspoon salt per quart of water plus 1 tablespoon oil to keep the pasta from sticking. Bring water to a boil, add the pasta and keep the heat high enough so that the water boils rapidly. (If water stops boiling cover the pot until water returns to a boil.) Stir the pasta occasionally to prevent it from sticking. Don't overcook your pasta, and don't trust the times printed on the box. Trust your taste buds. Start sampling dried pasta 4–5 minutes and fresh pasta 30 seconds after cooking starts. Pasta is best served firm yet tender (al dente, Italian for "to the teeth").

6. Mediterranean Tuna Salad Whisk together 3 tablespoons olive oil, 2 tablespoons lemon juice and 1 pressed garlic clove. Mix with 1 (6½ ounce) can drained, flaked tuna, 1 tablespoon drained capers, 1 cup drained cannellini beans and 2 tablespoons toasted pine nuts. Add salt and pepper to taste, and sprinkle with 2 tablespoons chopped, fresh parsley. You can also add 1 cup cubed, cooked new potatoes.

STRACCIATELLA

Much easier to prepare than pronounce, this sumptuous, light soup makes a terrific first course or a light supper when served with bread and salad.

> 2 eggs
> ¼ cup grated Parmesan cheese, plus more to top soup
> 2 tablespoons bread crumbs or Cream of Wheat
> ¼ teaspoon dried thyme
> 6 cups chicken broth, 3 (16 ounce) cans
> Freshly ground black pepper, to taste
> 1 tablespoon fresh parsley, finely minced

1. Beat together the eggs, cheese, bread crumbs or Cream of Wheat and thyme. Stir in 1 cup chicken broth.
2. In a medium-size saucepan, bring the remaining 5 cups broth to a boil. When the soup boils whisk in the egg mixture, stirring constantly so that egg forms thin ribbons. Reduce heat, cover and simmer for 5 minutes. Add the pepper and stir in parsley.
3. Serve immediately topped with additional grated cheese.

Variation: For a more substantial soup, add 1 cup cooked cheese tortellini to the boiling broth after adding the egg mixture.

LINGUINE WITH WHITE CLAM SAUCE

A delicious low-cal sauce that's ready quicker than you can cook pasta.

> 8 ounces linguine
> 1 tablespoon olive oil
> 1 medium onion, chopped
> 3 garlic cloves, minced
> 1 (8 ounce) bottle clam juice
> 2 (6 ½ ounce) cans chopped clams, drained, juice reserved
> 1 tablespoon cornstarch, mixed with 1 tablespoon water
> 1 cup evaporated milk
> ¼ cup grated Parmesan cheese, plus more to top pasta
> 1 tablespoon dried basil leaves

2 tablespoons fresh parsley, finely chopped
Salt and freshly ground black pepper, to taste

1. Boil water for the pasta. When the water boils cook linguine until al dente, about 8–10 minutes. If pasta is done before sauce, drain pasta, cover and set aside.

2. In large sauté pan, heat the olive oil over medium heat. Add the onion and sauté until soft, about 5 minutes. Add the garlic and sauté for another minute. Add the reserved and bottled clam juice. Bring to a boil over medium heat, and cook for a few minutes until liquid is reduced by half.

3. Whisk the cornstarch into the evaporated milk. Add to the pan, bring to a simmer, and cook, stirring continuously, until sauce thickens, about 2–3 minutes.

4. Add the chopped clams, Parmesan cheese, basil and parsley. Cook briefly until the clams are heated through. Add salt and pepper to taste. Serve over the cooked linguine topped with additional Parmesan cheese.

CAPER ARTICHOKE OLIVE SAUCE

Why settle for ordinary sauce when you can have extraordinary sauce?

2 cups prepared tomato sauce
2 tablespoons capers
2 tablespoons sliced black olives
8 ounces canned artichoke hearts, cut in quarters
1 teaspoon dried oregano
1 teaspoon dried basil
Freshly ground black pepper, to taste

1. Mix all ingredients in a medium saucepan. Bring to a simmer and serve over your favorite pasta.

PERFECT BAKED POTATOES

While the potatoes are baking, whip up several of our toppings.

4 large baking potatoes
Olive oil

1. Preheat oven to 400°F.

2. Scrub the potatoes and dry well. Pierce the potatoes several times with a fork, then coat all over with olive oil. Place right on the rack and bake until potatoes are soft, about 45–60 minutes.

3. Remove from oven. Cut open each potato and fill with one of the following mixtures or with an invention of your own.

- Top each spud with ½ cup heated chili and 1 tablespoon grated cheddar cheese.

- Top each spud with ½ cup steamed broccoli and 2 tablespoons grated cheddar cheese. Microwave for 1 minute on high to melt the cheese.

- Top each spud with 2 tablespoons sour cream and 1 tablespoon crumbled bacon, sprinkle with chopped chives.

- Sauté a chopped onion in 1 tablespoon oil for about 5–6 minutes. Add a chopped pepper (red or green) and ½ cup sliced mushrooms. Sauté until vegetables are soft. Then top each spud with ½ cup of mixture and grated Parmesan or Romano cheese.

- Mix ¼ cup feta cheese, 2 tablespoons chopped olives, 1 chopped tomato, ½ chopped roasted red pepper, 1 teaspoon balsamic vinegar, 1 tablespoon olive oil and ½ teaspoon Italian herbs. Top each spud with ½ cup of the mixture.

3

Spicing Up Romance

"A tale without love is like beef without mustard: insipid."

— *Anatole France*

*S*pices should be part of your pantry. "But all I've got is salt and pepper," you say. (And you ain't talkin' 'bout the rap group, Jack.) It's time to turn over a new leaf, especially if it's basil. One secret of being a great cook has nothing to do with talent or training and everything to do with ingredients. To establish your culinary reputation and leave your guests muttering jealously, keep an array of herbs and spices on hand and learn to use them.

Faking it in the kitchen, like faking it in the bedroom, doesn't work. You can buy a spice rack and prominently display jars of cumin, wasabi and fenugreek so everyone will think you are a gourmet cook; but if you don't know how to use them, eventually your date will ascertain your true culinary colors. Commit to conquering herbs and spices, and you won't need to explain yourself.

Remember, many spices and herbs are aphrodisiacs. Caraway and parsley are reputed to create a desire for sex. Anise, basil, cinnamon, clove, fennel, ginger, marjoram, rosemary and thyme are believed to bring love. Cardamom, coriander, licorice and vanilla are thought to promote love and lust.

Some people define herbs as leaves and spices as seeds, barks, roots, flowers and fruits. Others say spices come from tropical plants. Regardless of how you define them, spices have helped shape world history. Not very long ago men killed each other for cinnamon. Early in the sixteenth century the Portuguese savagely guarded the area from Oman to Goa, killing and enslaving anyone who made a move on their cinnamon bark. The great powers of Europe fought over the famed "Spice Routes" to the Far East. Nowadays, you only have to kill the pimple-faced punk with the nose ring who cut in front of you in the checkout line. Ah, the modern world.

We generally prefer fresh herbs to dried. They have more flavor and imbue dishes with a fresh, earthy fragrance. However, we use dried herbs, as well. They don't wilt and will keep for about a year if stored in airtight containers in a cool, dry place away from light. Fresh, cut herbs only keep for a few days. The best way to keep fresh herbs fresh is to grow them yourself and snip at leisure. But that's a different book, and since we don't find crawling around in backyard mud on a Saturday afternoon sexy, someone else can write that one. We'd rather picnic. If a recipe calls for fresh herbs, you can substitute about ½ teaspoon dried herbs for each teaspoon fresh.

Start your herb collection with our two favorite mixtures. Herbes de Provence, a blend of thyme, lavender, summer savory, basil and rosemary, that's great in salads, on chicken and in tomato-based dishes. And Italian

Seasoning, a blend of oregano, basil, savory, marjoram, rosemary, thyme and sage, that will transport you to Italy and send your pasta sauces soaring.

The basic dried herbs we keep on hand are:

Basil — Great in sauces, salad dressings, marinades, stews, tomato-based and cheese dishes. Use for pesto and to flavor herb butters. Some Latin cultures believe basil also squelches infidelity.

Bay Leaves — Use whole to flavor soups, stews and sauces. Make sure to remove the leaf before serving. You can choke on them, and that's no way to impress a date.

Oregano — Works well with basil. A must in Italian dishes. Great in tomato sauce, cheese and egg dishes, poultry and fish.

Rosemary — Has a clean, fresh, bittersweet taste. Use on roasted chicken, lamb and potatoes. Also works with fish and vegetable dishes. Sacred to Venus, the goddess of love.

Thyme — Very aromatic. Great in soups, stews, stuffings and salad dressings and on chicken, lamb and steak.

We use dill, chives and cilantro less often and usually buy fresh. We love the flavor of fresh parsley, so we purchase a bunch every week.

Cilantro — An important ingredient for certain Asian and Mexican dishes.

Chives — This herb has a delicate onion-like flavor. A must for baked or mashed potatoes especially with sour cream. Delicious in cream sauces, on fish and in dips.

Dill — Great on potatoes and fish dishes.

When it comes to spices, we prefer freshly ground because they are more flavorful and have a longer shelf life. Ground spices keep for about six

BASIC SPICE RUB

2 tablespoons kosher salt
2 tablespoons freshly ground
    black pepper
2 tablespoons brown sugar
1 tablespoon chili powder
1 tablespoon onion powder
1 teaspoon ground cumin
1 teaspoon cayenne pepper

Combine the following ingredients. Rub into poultry (try to get under the skin), pork or steak, let sit several hours or overnight for large cuts of meat before cooking. Use about 2 tablespoons per pound of meat. Store in a closed jar in a cool, dry, dark place.

SALT

Salt is essential for life and essential for enhancing the flavor of food. People crave salt, like they crave sugar and fat, and even have special taste buds to detect saltiness.

Salt has always been an important seasoning and preservative. It draws moisture from bacteria and mold, keeping food from spoiling. Salt was once a valuable commodity. Today, salt is cheap and plentiful, and most people consume much more than they need.

Salt is our most common and basic seasoning. It has no flavor, yet augments flavors. Salt also draws the bitterness from foods like eggplant.

Salt comes in different forms from fine table salt to coarse kosher, rock and sea salt. Since taste buds differ, most recipes suggest adding "salt to taste." When you salt food add a little at a time, taste and add more if necessary. Make sure to taste foods at the temperature you will serve them because very hot or cold foods can dull taste buds.

---

months. Whole spices last for up to two years. We also use preground spices for convenience. Our favorite spices and spice mixtures are:

Cayenne Pepper — From the dried red capsicum pepper (chili), a pinch adds a touch of heat.

Chili Powder — A mixture of cumin, ground chilies, salt, garlic and oregano used for Mexican dishes, especially chili.

Cinnamon — A robust spice used for sweet and savory dishes from baked apples and French toast to beef stew.

Cumin — Adds a pungent, spicy flavor to Indian, Latin American and Mexican dishes.

Curry Powder — A blend of cumin, coriander, turmeric and ginger.

Five-Spice Powder — A pungent blend of star anise, anise seed, clove, cinnamon and Szchuan peppercorns used in some Asian dishes.

Garam Masala — A spicy mix that contains black pepper, cloves and coriander. Essential in Indian cooking.

Ginger — A pungent root that's an essential ingredient in gingerbread and great in stir-fries.

Paprika — Like cayenne pepper, this spice also comes from ground chilies except it's milder. Generally, we sprinkle paprika on foods to add a little color.

When using herbs and spices, there are no strict rules, only good taste. Here are some suggestions to get you started. Herbs and spices can be added to most dishes including some desserts. (Try strawberries with a little freshly ground pepper.) To flavor grilled or roasted meat and poultry, rub herbs and spices (about 2 tablespoons per pound of meat) into flesh before cooking. For sauces and stews add herbs during the last 30 minutes of cooking, and save a few sprigs to toss on the dish right before serving. For other cooked dishes mince and add fresh herbs at the last minute so their flavor doesn't dissipate. Rub dried herbs between your fingers before using to release flavor.

Ground spices release their flavor quickly, so add them about 15 minutes before your dish is done, and don't forget to enjoy their fragrance and taste as you cook. To intensify flavor, roast spices in a dry skillet over medium heat, shaking the pan frequently, until they smoke slightly, about 2–3 minutes.

Avoid overpowering a dish. Think of herbs and spices as perfume for food. You don't want your food to reek; you want it to entice. Herbs and spices vary from batch to batch, so you may need to adjust seasonings. Season a little at a time, taste the dish, then add a bit more if necessary. Remember, spice dishes proportionally and keep it simple. If you do go overboard, there are several things you can do before ditching the stew and going out to eat. Try straining out the herbs or spices, add a peeled raw potato to absorb flavors or add more of the bland ingredients from the recipe.

Buy herbs and spices in small amounts. They lose flavor over time. Don't skimp on cheap powdered spices. Spend a few pennies more and get the real thing. The investment will be the difference between "Nice try" and "Wow, I can't believe you made this. It's better than a restaurant." And you know what? It will be.

PEPPER

Although not essential for health or taste, no kitchen is complete without a pepper mill. Like salt, pepper has influenced world history. Pepper was expensive yet indispensable for cooks throughout history. The Romans enjoyed the valuable spice, and Europeans began using pepper as early as the 5th or 6th century.

Pepper has little odor and therefore tends to strengthen dishes without masking flavors. It is added to foods from steak to strawberries.

Black peppercorns are under-ripened berries that have been picked and allowed to dry in the sun. White peppercorns are black peppercorns without the hull.

When we call for "pepper" in a recipe we mean freshly ground black pepper. There is no substitute for freshly ground pepper. Preground pepper loses its flavor too quickly. Besides, nothing adds a dash of panache like passing the pepper mill.

HERB CHEESE

This is a wonderful dip for vegetables or crackers. Try it in our recipes for Eggplant Sandwiches or Stuffed Mushrooms.

> **8 ounces cream cheese, softened**
> **2 tablespoons fresh herbs, chopped**
> **¼ cup fresh parsley, chopped**
> **1 tablespoon lemon juice**
> **Salt and freshly ground black pepper, to taste**

1. Mix all ingredients until smooth.

Variations: Substitute goat cheese for ½ the cream cheese. Or add a pressed garlic clove or 1 chopped scallion to the recipe.

EGGPLANT SANDWICHES

> **1 large eggplant**
> **1 egg, beaten with 1 tablespoon water**
> **¾ cup bread crumbs**

1. Slice the eggplant thinly, about ¼ inch. To remove bitterness, sprinkle the eggplant slices generously with salt, place slices in a colander between paper towels, weigh down with a heavy plate and let drain for about an hour. Rinse the eggplant slices with water and pat dry with paper towels.
2. Preheat oven to 350°F. Grease a baking sheet.
3. Dip eggplant slices, one at a time, into the egg mixture and then into the bread crumbs. Place on prepared baking sheet and bake until slices are soft and golden brown, about 30 minutes.
4. Spread generously with Herb Cheese.

CREAMY SQUASH SOUP

This soup works well as a first course or light supper. You can make it ahead of time and reheat before serving.

1 tablespoon vegetable oil
1 medium onion, chopped
1 large or 2 small winter squash, such as butternut, about 3 pounds
3 cups chicken broth
1 cup milk
¼ teaspoon cayenne pepper
¼ teaspoon dried thyme
Salt and freshly ground black pepper, to taste
Paprika
Yogurt, sour cream or toasted slivered almonds, for garnish

1. Heat the oil in a large stockpot over medium heat. Add the onion and sauté until soft, about 5–6 minutes.

2. Peel the squash, remove seeds and cut into 1-inch cubes. Add to the stockpot along with the chicken broth. Bring to a boil, reduce heat, cover and simmer until the squash is soft, about 30 minutes.

3. Purée the soup in a blender or food processor. (You may need to do this in several batches.)

4. Return soup to stockpot. Stir in the milk, cayenne pepper and thyme. Simmer gently over low heat. Add salt and pepper to taste. You can add 1 teaspoon brown sugar to make the soup slightly sweeter.

5. To serve, ladle the soup into bowls, sprinkle with paprika and top with yogurt, sour cream or slivered almonds.

Variation: Replace the cayenne pepper and thyme with ¼ teaspoon nutmeg, ¼ teaspoon ginger and ¼ teaspoon cinnamon.

INDIAN PILLOWS

These require a little work, but they are guaranteed to have your date eating out of your hands. You can make them a few hours ahead and reheat them.

2 medium-size potatoes
1 tablespoon vegetable oil
1 medium-size onion, chopped
1 teaspoon fresh gingerroot, grated
½ teaspoon ground coriander
½ teaspoon garam masala
½ teaspoon ground cumin
⅛ teaspoon cayenne pepper, or to taste
½ cup frozen peas
1 medium carrot, chopped
Salt, to taste
½ package phyllo dough (12 sheets)
¼ cup olive oil

1. Peel the potatoes, cut into chunks and boil until tender. Let potatoes cool and cut into ¼-inch dice.

2. Heat 1 tablespoon vegetable oil in skillet over medium heat. Add the onion and sauté until soft, about 5 minutes. Add the gingerroot, coriander, garam masala, cumin and cayenne and cook for another minute.

3. Add the peas, carrot and 2 tablespoons water. Cover, reduce heat and simmer, stirring occasionally and adding a little water if mixture starts to get dry, until carrot is tender, about 5 minutes. Stir in the cooked potatoes, add salt to taste and remove from the burner.

4. Preheat over to 350°F. Grease a baking sheet. Uncover the phyllo dough. (Keep remaining dough covered with a damp cloth so it doesn't dry out.) On a large cutting board, lay out one sheet phyllo dough, and using a pastry brush, paint on a thin layer of olive oil. Cover with another sheet of dough and another layer of olive oil. Repeat for a third sheet of dough.

5. Cut the dough into three strips, lengthwise, with a sharp knife. Place about 2 tablespoons filling at the end of each strip. Fold a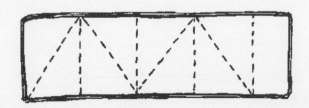

corner across filling and continue folding (as if you were folding a flag) until entire strip is folded and you have a triangle. Place on baking sheet. Repeat with remaining dough.

    6. Brush pillows with additional olive oil. Bake until golden brown, about 25 minutes.

ONION HERB BREAD

Easy and guaranteed to impress. It's so good that you might not get to dinner.

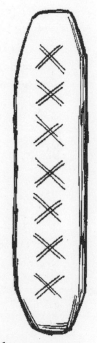

    1 pound prepared bread or pizza dough, fresh or frozen*
    1 tablespoon olive oil
    1 medium onion, chopped
    2 tablespoons herbes de Provence
    ¼ cup Parmesan cheese
    1 egg, beaten with 1 tablespoon water

    1. Defrost the bread dough, if necessary.

    2. Heat the oil in sauté pan over medium heat, and sauté onion until soft, about 5–6 minutes.

    3. Combine sautéed onion, herbs and cheese.

    4. Lightly grease a baking sheet. Stretch dough out into a rectangle approximately 10 x 12-inches. Spread with onion, cheese, herb mixture. Roll dough up the long way starting at the 12-inch end. Place on prepared baking sheet. Brush with the beaten egg. Cover the bread with plastic wrap, set in warm place and let bread rise for 30–45 minutes.

    5. Preheat oven to 350°F. Cut a few slits, about 1-inch deep, in the top of the bread to let steam escape during baking. Bake until bread is golden brown and sounds hollow when you tap it, about 30 minutes.

Variation: Use 2 tablespoons rosemary and ¼ cup chopped sun-dried tomatoes that have been reconstituted in boiling water for a few minutes, instead of the herbes de Provence. You can also add ¼ cup sliced black olives in addition to or instead of the tomatoes.

Raw pizza dough is available at many pizzerias and also in the refrigerator or freezer section of grocery stores.

4

Getting to Know You

"I don't know how to kiss, or I would kiss you.
Where do the noses go?"

— *Ingrid Bergman to Gary Cooper
in* For Whom the Bell Tolls

T.G.I.F. The deal with J Corp. Products went sour. On Monday you were 30 minutes late to work because you couldn't find parking, and on Thursday you got a speeding ticket for doing 40 in a 39 miles-per-hour zone. Who cares! The weekend's almost here. You have a date with the dream boat you met at that swanky, downtown club two weeks ago. You both like beer, Kafka and contra dancing. Could this be love?

Push away the papers, let the phone ring and dream about the dream boat. Picture your date's face. Remember that first kiss? Get excited, you're seeing your new beau tonight.

TONIGHT! Oh God. Your daydream turns to nightmare. You promised to cook dinner. Panic time. You haven't done a thing. The apartment is a disaster. The litter box hasn't been changed in over a month, and the cat's been using the people toilet. You forgot to take out the garbage on Tuesday and can't remember the last time the bathtub was scrubbed. Was it ever scrubbed? "Maybe I should tell him/her I have to work late. Maybe we can do it next week, next month, next year. No, I'll tell him/her I've been drafted."

Relax. Take a deep breath. This is your first Friday night dinner. Don't let it be the last supper. Grab the yellow pages, turn to "House Cleaning" and DIAL! The Merry Maids can be at your apartment by 2:00 p.m.

Time to focus on dinner. You're date's coming at 7:30, you've got plenty of time. Go food shopping during lunch. Actually, tell your boss you have an excruciating migraine and sneak out early. You weren't planning on getting any work done today anyway. On your way home don't forget to stop at the cleaners and pick up your outfit.

Being nervous is natural, especially if you think you're cooking for Mr. or Ms. Right. The first time I made dinner for Michael, I was anxious. He called me two days after our second date and asked if I wanted to see Graham Parker.

"Graham who?" Why were we going to see a cracker, I wondered.
"Graham Parker," he repeated. *"Wanna go?"*
"I'd love to," I said, still not knowing who Graham Parker was.

Later, I discovered Michael had stood up a tattooed-blond violinist for me. I offered to make dinner for him before the show. Good thing I could really cook. My mother taught me about pots and pans before the birds and bees. Dad taught me about algebra and amino acids, but that's another book.

Maybe it was the succulent chicken or the bottle of chardonnay. Perhaps it was the bluesy love ballads that Graham seemed to be singing just for the two of us. The night was a fabulous swirl that went on forever. That fateful eve, we stopped dating and became eternal lovers.

As far as we're concerned a relationship doesn't start until you've sealed the alliance with a kiss and a home-cooked meal. We don't care if you've slept together, are contemplating buying a puppy or are planning to be roommates in Paris. Without that first meal you can't call yourself a couple.

We know what you're thinking, "I'm a disaster in the kitchen." Bury your culinary past with the burnt rice. Learning to cook is like learning to walk. Everyone can do it. Some learn faster, but you're not trying to win a race. All you need to do is cross this bridge in your relationship, and we're going to support you with a selection of easy, foolproof recipes. Still petrified? Take time to plan your menu and practice on a roommate or tolerant friend. Whatever you make, your first meal, like your first step, will be memorable.

If you want your date to break out in goose bumps, not hives, and be short of breath because of you, not your mushroom stew, make sure to find out if they have any food allergies. (Mushrooms, fish, especially shellfish, chocolate, tomatoes, peanuts, milk and eggs are common allergens.) Chances are your date will not have a physical reaction to shrimp in peanut sauce. But who wants a comatose guest before dessert? So ask.

Also ask if your date is a vegetarian. Many people who call themselves vegetarians simply don't eat red meat but do eat poultry or fish. If your date is a vegetarian, turn to Chapter 15 "Where's the Beef?"

If your date's dieting tell your new beau "your body's great," and hope this will get him/her off the diet and into bed. If your date needs to lose weight and isn't a Kate Moss wanna be whose idea of a good dinner is celery, mineral water and two Marlboros, be supportive and cook one of our lighter recipes. Remember, it's the love you put into the meal that makes it great, not the fat.

A hint: Avoid frogs' legs (they may remind your date of high school biology class), stewed rabbit and squid. Save rabbit for the petting zoo and squid for catching fish. Before serving fish or beef, find out if your date eats them. Many people dislike fish and others feel beef causes instantaneous cardiac arrest. Chicken is the safest first date dish for carnivores. Most people like it, there are no religious taboos surrounding chicken, people generally feel poultry is healthy and it's easy to prepare.

The first few dates are the perfect time to discuss food and discover what your potential partner prefers. When you go to a restaurant, observe your date's eating habits. Does your date relish food or appear indifferent? If your

IN CASE YOU WERE WONDERING

We don't recommend serving unusual meats on the first date. Why take a chance? But in case you were wondering what snake, rabbit, alligator, iguana, frogs' legs and turtle all taste like...that's right chicken. And ostrich resembles red meat, except it's much, much lower in fat and cholesterol.

Don't even think about serving variety meats — brains, chitterlings (the large intestines of pigs), ears, feet, fries (testicles), gizzards, heads, sweetbrains (the thymus gland of calves or young lambs), tail, tongue and tripe (cow stomach lining), unless your date is from France. These "delicacies" are called "offal" for a reason.

date doesn't know the difference between chipped beef on toast and chateaubriand, think about this relationship before it goes too far. Do you want to live on bologna, Cheese Whiz and tuna noodle casserole for the rest of your life?

Perhaps you can transform your date with your magic wooden spoon and a drop of chocolate. But don't count on it. Some people see food only as fuel for the body, ignoring its significance to their soul and psyche. If you're serious about food and your date's not, don't let the relationship get too serious. Humor them as they munch on their fifth frozen Taco Bob with extra mayo, and start looking for a mate with better taste.

If you're a great cook, don't make anything too elaborate the first night. You want your date to fall in love with you, not your cooking. Keep it simple.

Other Cooking Couple do's and don'ts for that first dinner are: ALWAYS give your roommate $10.00 to get lost and go to the movies. Nothing's worse than having your roommate march into the kitchen wearing only a bathrobe and panties or boxer shorts and a T-shirt from a college they weren't smart enough to get into and start a conversation with your dream boat. Roommates and dates don't mix. So get rid of them (the roommate, not the date), and lose the Fabio or Playmate-of-the-Month poster. Leave Fido outside with Fabio. Although not as annoying as your half-naked roommate, your dog may take a liking to (or start licking) your date and upstage dinner. Make sure the dishes and silverware are clean. In fact, make sure you have dishes and silverware. Buy some nice napkins, flowers and candles. Don't forget wine. After a few glasses, conversation starts to flow, and food always tastes better with a touch of the heavenly grape.

ROAST CHICKEN

You can't go wrong with roast chicken (unless you forget to pull it out of the freezer), especially if you use a chicken with a pop-up thermometer.

2 tablespoons olive oil
2 tablespoons fresh lemon juice
2 garlic cloves, minced
1 teaspoon herbes de Provence
1 whole roasting chicken
Salt and freshly ground black pepper, to taste
1 medium carrot, chopped
1 medium onion, chopped

1. Preheat the oven to 450°F.

2. Mix the olive oil, lemon juice, garlic and ½ teaspoon herbes de Provence.

3. Remove giblets, rinse the chicken well, both inside and out and pat dry. Season the inside cavity and outside of chicken with salt and pepper. Sprinkle the chopped carrot, chopped onion and remaining ½ teaspoon herbes de Provence inside the cavity.

4. Put chicken on a rack in a roasting pan, breast side up. Brush the outside of the chicken with the olive oil, lemon juice, garlic and herb mixture. Set remaining olive oil and lemon juice mixture aside to baste chicken during cooking.

5. Place the chicken in the middle of the lower rack in preheated oven and immediately turn oven down to 350°F. Baste about every 20 minutes. Chicken is done when pop-up timer pops or when juices run clear when a skewer is inserted into the thickest part of the thigh, 1–1½ hours depending on size of bird (about 20 minutes per pound plus an extra 20 minutes if you are stuffing the bird).

6. Let chicken rest for about 10 minutes before carving.

CONFETTI RICE

You can use this rice as a side dish or a stuffing for roast chicken. If you use Confetti Rice as a stuffing, omit sprinkling cavity with carrot and onion, and fill the chicken loosely with the cooked rice right before roasting.

> 2 tablespoons butter
> 1 medium onion, chopped
> ½ cup pine nuts or slivered almonds
> 1 cup long grain white rice
> 2 cups chicken broth
> ½ cup raisins
> ¼ teaspoon cinnamon
> Salt and freshly ground pepper, to taste

1. Melt the butter in a saucepan over medium heat and sauté onion until soft, about 5–6 minutes.

2. Toast the nuts by placing them in a 350°F oven and stirring frequently until nuts are golden, about 6–7 minutes.

3. When the onions are cooked, add the rice and sauté for 2–3 minutes, stirring frequently.

4. Add the chicken broth, raisins and cinnamon. Turn the heat up to high and bring to a boil.

5. Reduce the heat to low, cover and simmer until liquid is absorbed, about 20 minutes. Stir in nuts and salt and pepper to taste. Serve or use for stuffing chicken.

FISH DELIGHT

Impressing a date has never been easier. Just sprinkle fish with salt, pepper, lemon juice, thyme and garlic, and bake it. Serve with white rice and steamed broccoli or green beans. Try baking fish with Mustard Sauce (recipe follows).

¼ cup dry white wine or vermouth
1 pound white fish filet, such as cod, haddock or scrod
2 tablespoons lemon juice
2 garlic cloves, minced
½ teaspoon dried thyme
Salt and freshly ground black pepper, to taste
Mustard Sauce, optional, recipe follows
2 tablespoons parsley, minced
Lemon wedges, for garnish

1. Preheat oven to 350°F.
2. Grease a pan large enough to hold the fish. Pour the wine into the pan.
3. Sprinkle the fish fillets with the lemon juice, garlic, thyme, salt and pepper.
4. Place fish in prepared pan. Spread the fish generously with the Mustard Sauce, if you are using it. Cover the pan with foil to keep the fish from drying out.
5. Bake until the fish flakes easily with a fork and flesh turns from translucent to white, about 20–35 minutes depending on thickness of fish. Sprinkle with parsley and garnish with lemon wedges.

MUSTARD SAUCE

An elegant sauce for chicken or fish that you can whip up in minutes.

> 2 tablespoons Dijon mustard
> 1 tablespoon fresh lemon juice
> ¼ teaspoon sugar
> ⅛ teaspoon freshly ground black pepper
> ⅓ cup mayonnaise

1. Combine the mustard, lemon juice, sugar, pepper and mayonnaise.

2. If using for fish recipe, spread several spoonfuls Mustard Sauce over the fish after seasoning with garlic, thyme, salt and pepper.

5

Champagne Saturday

"The best defense against the rain?
Get back in bed and open champagne."
— *The Cooking Couple*

*D*on't let a little drizzle dampen your mood. Rain provides the perfect excuse to escape for the afternoon and drift into a long foggy evening. Forget the ball game, shopping and laundry. You don't want to be out in this weather anyway. Grab your sweetheart, jump back in bed and pop the cork.

We hope you've incorporated The Cooking Couple philosophy and have the proper ingredients on hand: champagne, bread, cheese and chocolate. If you're not prepared, turn back to "Passion-Filled Pantry" and get to the store before the rain sets in. Fantasize and prepare ahead of time so your body, soul and pantry will be ready. After a love-filled afternoon, the last thing you'll want to do is get dressed and visit a store to forage for food.

This plan works best as a mid-afternoon, predinner prelude. When it looks like the weather isn't getting better, stop what you're doing and turn on romantic music. We suggest cool jazz. Frank Morgan harmonizes particularly well with the pitter-patter of rain. If you have a CD player, set it on repeat. Once while researching this chapter, we stayed in bed until the sun had set and *Saturday Night Live* was about to start. The only thing reminding us of passing time was the repeating CD. The only things urging us out of bed were growling stomachs.

Silently take your partner's hand, ignoring foul moods, questions and protests. Don't worry: This scenario has been tested on the grumpiest lovers. Twirl your sweetie around the living room and waltz into the kitchen. Grab your chilled champagne, a cooler or bucket of ice and two glasses. Lead your lover to bed. Carrying your partner is a nice touch if you're strong enough. But if you haven't been to the gym lately, don't even think about it. Dropping your mate is *not* romantic. In fact, it's the best contraceptive we know. Nothing like a bruised spine to break the mood.

When you have your lover in bed, pour two glasses of champagne, then two more and then two more and let nature take its course. Trust us, it will. Ah, the wonders of nature. Soon you'll be champagne saturated and sexually satiated. No matter how relaxed you are, eventually you'll pull your groggy selves out of bed and discover that you're famished. (Michael refuses to go to bed hungry. Sometimes when he waits too long to eat, he gets delirious and starts singing *Food Glorious Food* from *Oliver*. He's very cute, especially if you like watching naked men jump around the bed performing Broadway show tunes.)

Relax. If you follow our instructions, a feast will be ready in minutes. After an afternoon of love, any food should taste wonderful. A simple feast of cheese, bread and chocolate will be heaven. Want to dazzle your lover? Try our delicious bacon-wrapped tidbits. After eating these you'll know why we call them Love Bites. If caviar is your love food, open another bottle of champagne, and try our recipe for Caviar Topped Potatoes. Both recipes are easy and fun to prepare together. For your dining pleasure, we've also include recipes for elegant Smoked Salmon Penne and Chocolate Dipped Strawberries. Of course, if you want to dazzle your date one more time and lure them back to bed, oysters, a well know aphrodisiac, aren't a bad idea.

For after-dinner entertainment *Casablanca* is your best ticket. The black and white version only. Watching the colorized monstrosity is like putting ketchup on a steak from Morton's. Even if you've seen it before, drunk on love and champagne you'll appreciate the film with new eyes. "Of all the gin joints in the world why did she have to walk into mine?" "I remember it well, you

---

CLASS IN A GLASS

Champagne makes any time of the day or night special, and it doesn't have to cost big bucks. Our favorite champagne is Moët White Star. If you shop around you can find it in the low $20s. Sometimes it can be had for as little as $19. Find a brand you like and can afford. Then buy a case so you'll always have a bottle ready to fire romance.

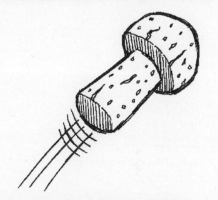

Champagne refers to both a place (the Province of Champagne that lies about 90 miles west of Paris where champagne is produced) and a process. Unlike regular wine, champagne is allowed to ferment both before and after bottling. The gas given off after bottling dissolves in the wine, resulting in bubbles. Because of the bubbles, the alcohol in champagne enters the blood stream rapidly, resulting in a quick buzz.

Champagne tastes best alone or with light foods such as shrimp, caviar or brie, although Marlene Dietrich's favorite meal was champagne and hot dogs.

The only rules, when enjoying champagne are serve it chilled and, when you open the bottle, point the cork away from yourself and your date. To open champagne like a pro, remove the wire, wrap a towel around the cork, turn and slowly ease out the cork so it doesn't fly and hit someone. On the other hand, if you're feeling like a 12-year-old, let it rip.

wore blue…the Germans wore gray." "Look Ilsa, we don't have much time." "You played it for her, you can play it for me. I can take it." "Round up the usual suspects." Don't break the moment: Pull the T.V. into the bedroom and feast on the world's most romantic film. "Here's lookin' at you kid." If you prefer more tension with your romance, then try Alfred Hitchcock's *Notorious* with Cary Grant and Ingrid Bergman. It's *Casablanca* with an S&M twist.

Of course you may choose to watch T.V. *and* eat in bed. In that case serve dinner in the boudoir, feast on succulent finger food, wipe the crumbs from your lips, make love again and fall asleep wrapped in your lover's arms.

SMOKED SALMON PENNE

After trying our Smoked Salmon Penne, you'll know why we recommend keeping a stash of smoked salmon in the freezer at all times.

8 ounces penne
3 tablespoons butter
3 tablespoons flour
1½ cups milk, warmed in microwave or over low heat
¼ cup grated Parmesan cheese, plus additional to top pasta
½ cup frozen peas, defrosted
Salt and white pepper, to taste
4 ounces smoked salmon, cut into ½-inch pieces

1. Bring pasta water to a boil, add the penne and cook pasta until al dente. Drain the pasta. If the pasta is ready before the sauce, keep pasta warm in a covered pan until ready to serve.

2. In a medium saucepan, melt the butter over low heat. When butter melts and starts to bubble, whisk in the flour, 1 tablespoon at a time. Continue to stir mixture over low heat for 3 minutes completely combining butter and flour.

3. Turn heat up to medium. Stirring constantly with a wire whisk, slowly add the warm milk making sure to incorporate all of the flour/butter mixture. Continue to stir until sauce is thick, about 5 minutes.

4. Stir in the Parmesan cheese. Add the peas, salt and white pepper and cook until peas are heated through.

5. Stir in the smoked salmon. Toss sauce with pasta and serve with additional grated Parmesan cheese.

CAVIAR TOPPED POTATOES

If you have the budget, splurge on expensive, imported, beluga caviar and enjoy it by the spoonful with a bottle of champagne or chilled vodka. If you can't afford to spend a day's pay on caviar, buy a few ounces of less-expensive salmon or whitefish (American golden) caviar, and you'll still dazzle your date.

> 1 dozen tiny new red potatoes (about 1 pound)
> 1 tablespoon butter, melted
> ⅔ cup sour cream
> 2–3 ounces caviar
> Lemon juice

1. Preheat oven to 375°F.

2. Wash, scrub and dry the potatoes. Coat the potatoes with the butter and set on a baking sheet. Bake until the potatoes feel tender when pierced with a fork, about 30–45 minutes.

3. Let the potatoes cool slightly so you can handle them without burning your fingers. Cut the potatoes in half. Scoop out about a teaspoonful of pulp from each potato half.

4. Fill the potato halves with about 1 teaspoon sour cream. Top with caviar and drizzle with a few drops lemon juice. Leftover caviar is wonderful spread on buttered toast or used to top scrambled eggs.

LOVE BITES

We love Oysters Rockefeller and oysters on the half shell when someone else does the shucking. (Other cookbook writers may tell you that shucking oysters is easy. They lie.) The last thing you'll want to do after a champagne filled afternoon is try to get these little babies apart. So take our advice, chuck shucking and make our simple, delectable oyster bites.

> 1 dozen shucked oysters or 1 jar oysters (about 8 ounces)
> 2–3 slices bacon

1. Drain oysters.
2. Cut bacon into strips large enough to wrap around the oysters.
3. Wrap bacon around oysters and secure with a toothpick. Arrange on broiler pan.
4. Preheat broiler. Broil oysters, turning once, until bacon is crisp, about 3 minutes.

Variation: Instead of shucked oysters, try raw mussels, raw sea scallops, cooked shrimp, smoked oysters, smoked mussels, smoked clams, smoked ham, smoked turkey, sliced parakeet, water chestnuts dipped in soy sauce, quartered artichoke hearts, pickled onions, olives, pineapple chunks or pitted dates.

> *"What do you mean parakeet?"*
> *"I was just kidding. I wanted to make sure you were reading closely."*

CHOCOLATE DIPPED STRAWBERRIES

The only way to close Champagne Saturday as far as Ellen is concerned. Give these to your lover instead of long-stem roses and spend what you save on caviar.

> **2 dozen long-stem strawberries**
> **8 ounces chocolate (white, dark, bittersweet or semisweet), chopped**

1. Wash and completely dry strawberries.

2. Melt the chocolate in the top of a double boiler. (Water should be about 1-inch away from the top of the double boiler and hot, but NOT boiling.) Heat, stirring constantly, until the chocolate is just barely melted. Or melt the chocolate in a glass bowl over medium or high power in a microwave, stopping to stir every 30 seconds, until the chocolate is smooth, about 2–3 minutes.

3. Hold the strawberries by their stems, dip into the chocolate and let excess chocolate run off. Place on aluminum foil and enjoy. These can be refrigerated for a day, but they won't last that long.

Variation: Try dipping other types of fresh fruit — raspberries, tangerines and bananas work well — dried fruits, nuts, biscotti, pound cake, graham crackers or pretzels. Use a small fork or toothpick to hold fruit while dipping.

6

Sunday Brunch

"All the things I really like to do are either immoral, illegal or fattening."

— *Alexander Woollcott*

*W*ith mimosas flowing and kisses flying, brunch is the happiest meal of
the week. If muffins are baking, it's heaven on earth. Forget calories,
cholesterol and chores. RELAX. Enjoy the Sunday paper, go jogging or stay in
bed till noon. Rekindle Saturday night with a few transitions: jazz for rock
and roll, Moët for Rolling Rock, the crossword puzzle for club hopping.

Ambience and attitude are as important as food. Billie Holiday and Frank
Sinatra hit the right notes for a jazz brunch, Bach and Mozart for the classical
epicurean. The first warm days of spring demand an alfresco brunch on your
lawn, patio, fire escape or windowsill. The long cold days of winter demand a
fire and cognac.

Not ready to face daylight? Close the blinds and light candles. Dine in
your bathrobe (it makes nibbling easier) or stay in bed and eat in your
birthday suit. Keep a small cooler next to your bed so you won't have to get
up. Stock it with champagne, orange juice, grapes or strawberries (sour cream
and brown sugar for dipping are great additions), cream cheese, smoked
salmon, brie and butter to top bagels or crackers. Sound decadent? That's the
point.

Cooking brunch should be easy. Don't waste time on béarnaise sauce or
crepes suzette, unless you don't have a full-time job. Breaking eggs shouldn't
break the mood. Scramble four or five eggs, throw in a little (or a lot) of ham
and cheese. Serve rolled in tortillas with salsa. Elevate poached eggs by placing
them on a pedestal of toast and covering them with our quick, Easy
Hollandaise Sauce. Practice making omelettes, and don't worry if they look
like a bad Picasso. You've seen each other at your worst. A messy omelette isn't
going to change your date's opinion of you. And if it does, it's time to change
partners. Besides, messy omelettes taste better.

Toss a kiwi in the fruit salad and a splash of kahlua in your coffee. Toast
waffles and serve with berries and whipped cream. If you'd rather have ice
cream, go ahead, it's Sunday. Try a New York classic, fresh bagels with smoked
salmon and cream cheese, or our take on this traditional winning combination, Lox Latkes. Or enjoy Chocolate Bread Pudding, a Cooking Couple
favorite, 24 hours a day.

Too groggy to cook? Go for Saturday night's leftovers. Cold pizza is
delicious and Chinese food always tastes great the next day. Why? Who cares?
Just get that puppy in the microwave and dig into that MSG buzz with your
coffee, a truly psychedelic delight. Slice last-night's baked potatoes, sauté in a
little butter, pour in 5 or 6 beaten eggs, top with cheese, stick under the broiler
for a few minutes and call it a "frittata." That's Italian for omelette.

If you're looking to cap a hot Saturday night with a warm Sunday
morning, then don't neglect the beverage department. You drink office sludge

THE SPICE THAT LAUNCHED A THOUSAND SHIPS

One of the most popular spices of all time, clove was probably first used around 200 B.C. by the Chinese. The Greeks and Romans followed, and the Turks and Moors carefully kept the origin of clove a secret to maintain a monopoly on the market. Cloves were believed to have medicinal powers and still have a reputation as a powerful love food.

Cloves are the closed, dried bud of the tropical clove tree. Whole cloves are shaped like tacks. (The word "clove" comes from the Roman word for tack, "clovis.") They should be removed before serving a dish.

Whole cloves are frequently stuck in onions to flavor them before cooking. Cloves are also available in powdered form for adding to curries, spicy meat dishes and fruit compotes.

---

five days a week, Sunday coffee should be special. Try Café au Lait. Brew a pot of strong coffee (See "Coffee, Tea or…") and microwave 1 cup milk on high for 1 minute. (The milk will heat up without burning.) Fill a warmed mug halfway with coffee and top with ½ cup heated milk. Sprinkle with ground cinnamon or shaved chocolate. If you like strong, dark coffee spiked with chocolate, try Cioccolata. Brew espresso coffee and top with hot chocolate instead of plain milk. For Mexican Coffee brew two cups of strong hot coffee, add 1 teaspoon chocolate syrup and top with whipped cream and a dash of cinnamon and nutmeg.

Feel like imbibing? Add a dash of Tia Maria to your Mexican coffee or try some of the following brews. For Irish Coffee, brew a pot of strong coffee, add a shot of Irish cream liqueur and top with whipped cream. For a sophisticated

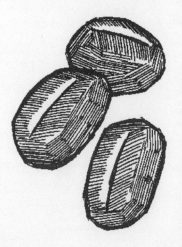

cup with a sense of drama, try Café Brûlot. In a saucepan combine 2 shots cognac or brandy, 2 whole cloves, 2 teaspoons sugar and 1 tablespoon sliced lemon or orange peel. Set pan over medium heat and stir until sugar dissolves. Ignite liquid (use a long match) and pour in 1 cup very strong, hot black coffee. Pour mixture into two mugs, straining out cloves, and serve with cinnamon sticks. Like playing with fire? Try Café Royal. It's a little less involved than Café Brûlot, but just as dramatic. Fill a spoon with cognac, place a sugar cube on the spoon, ignite and drop in hot coffee. For Spanish Coffee, mix 1 teaspoon

THE PERFECT MIMOSA

Fill champagne glass 1/2 to 2/3 full with champagne (depending on how much you plan to accomplish that day). Top with orange juice (preferably fresh squeezed). Garnish with a strawberry or an orange wedge. If you are out of orange juice, DO NOT use grapefruit juice. Run to the mini mart, or drink the champagne straight.

sugar with a shot of cointreau and ¼ teaspoon grated orange peel and top with coffee. Only have rum? Add a shot to your coffee, top with whipped cream and cinnamon and call it Café Viennoise.

After coffee, try our Secret Sparkling Mimosas. They go down like creamsicles and tickle your nose. Your playmate will think he/she died and went to *Lifestyles of the Rich and Famous.* There are three important secrets for success. Secret # 1: Use cheap champagne and lots of it. Don't spend a penny more than $10.00 per bottle. Secret #2: Mimosas at 11:00 a.m. ensure no work and lots of play even for type A personalities. Any earlier than 11:00, and you're either still awake from last night or Keith Richards is your bedmate. Secret # 3: You can't save champagne so you have to drink the whole thing. Which leads to The Cooking Couple's classically decadent, don't get out of bed, don't answer the phone, slide a little closer honey, oh that feels so goooooood kinda day.

THE PERFECT OMELETTE

Whipping up an outstanding omelette is one sign of a great chef. With practice you too will be able to shake your pan like a pro.

2–3 eggs
1 teaspoon water or milk
Salt and freshly ground black pepper, to taste
1 tablespoon butter

1. Break 2–3 eggs into a bowl. Add the water or milk if you like your eggs fluffy and salt and pepper to taste. Stir with a fork to combine yolk and white.

2. Heat a large skillet (about 10-inches) over medium-high heat. Drop in the butter. When the butter stops foaming, pour in the eggs. Gently stir the eggs around with a fork or plastic utensil, if you're using a nonstick pan. Lift the omelette pan off the burner to keep the eggs from getting too hot. When the omelette starts to set, lift an edge and allow some of the raw egg to run underneath. Then, add your filling (about ¼ cup) and return the skillet to the burner. Let the omelette cook for a minute to give the filling a chance to set. Fold the omelette in half, or roll both edges over the middle if you like 'em long and thin. Allow another minute for the filling to set, then slide omelette from pan directly onto plate.

3. Top with an additional ¼ cup filling.

Filling suggestions:
- Chopped fresh herbs
- Sautéed mushrooms and Swiss cheese
- Mixed sautéed vegetables (broccoli, spinach, peppers, etc.) and cheddar cheese
- Chopped tomato and mozzarella cheese
- Salsa, cheddar and avocado
- Bacon and onion
- Western (ham, cheese, onions and green peppers)
- Egg Foo Young (bean sprouts, sliced scallions, cooked shrimp, pork or chicken and a dash of soy sauce)

Mix and match any of these fillings or anything else you think might taste good, making sure to warm fillings slightly before adding to omelette. That's the beauty of an omelette. Think of the eggs as a blanket around your favorite cheeses, vegetables, meats or leftovers.

LOX LATKAS

These also make wonderful appetizers or grazing tray additions.

    3 tablespoons cream cheese
    ¼ cup sour cream
    2 tablespoons lemon juice
    1 pound baking potatoes (2–3), peeled
    2 tablespoons flour
    ½ teaspoon salt
    ⅛ teaspoon white pepper
    1 tablespoon butter, melted
    1 egg, beaten
    1 tablespoon vegetable oil
    4 ounces lox (smoked salmon)
    Sprigs of dill, for garnish

1. Mix together the cream cheese, sour cream and lemon juice until smooth.

2. Using a food processor or grater, shred the potatoes into a large bowl. Add the flour, salt, pepper, butter and egg. Mix well.

3. Heat the oven to 450°F. Grease a cookie sheet very well with the vegetable oil. Drop about ¼ cup of the potato mixture onto the prepared cookie sheet and press down lightly to form a pancake. Bake until bottom of the latkes are golden brown, about 10 minutes. Flip the latkes and bake until both sides are golden brown, about 5 minutes more.

4. Spread the cream cheese mixture on latkes. Top with the lox and sprinkle with dill.

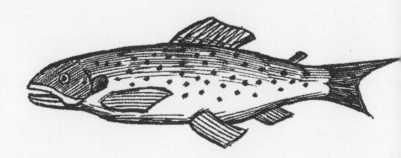

EASY HOLLANDAISE SAUCE

Perfect over poached eggs, vegetables, chicken or fish.

    2 egg yolks, brought to room temperature
    Pinch of cayenne pepper
    1 stick butter
    Salt and white pepper, to taste
    1 teaspoon fresh lemon juice

1. Mix the egg yolks, cayenne pepper and 2 teaspoons water in a food processor or blender.
2. Melt the butter over low heat. Skim off and discard the white solid material that floats to the top. Continue to heat the butter until it starts to boil slightly. Turn the food processor or blender on and add a few drops of the butter through the top. After you have added about one-third of the butter, with the motor running, slowly pour in the rest of the butter.
3. Add the lemon juice and salt and pepper to taste. Serve immediately.

CHOCOLATE BREAD PUDDING

If you're aiming to be extra decadent, this is just the ticket, especially when served with ice cream.

    12 slices challah or other firm white bread, such as Italian
    ½ stick unsalted butter
    2 cups milk
    6 eggs
    Pinch of salt
    1 cup chocolate chips
    ½ cup granulated sugar

1. Preheat the oven to 375°F. Butter a 1½ quart soufflé dish.
2. Cut the bread slices into quarters.
3. Melt the butter over low heat. In a bowl stir together the milk, eggs, butter and salt.
4. Place one-third of the bread pieces in the soufflé dish. Cover with one-third of the milk/egg mixture (about 1 cup). Sprinkle with half the chocolate chips (½ cup) and 2 tablespoons sugar. Repeat for another layer. For the top layer use the remaining bread, milk mixture and sugar but no chocolate chips.
5. Cover with foil. Bake for about 50 minutes until pudding is firm. Remove foil and cook until pudding is golden brown, about 10 more minutes.

PEARS FOSTER

This classic dish, originally created in the 1950s in New Orleans, is usually made with bananas. Here's our interpretation using pears.

2 pears
2 tablespoons butter
2 tablespoons brown sugar
⅛ teaspoon cinnamon
¼ cup dark rum
1 pint vanilla ice cream

1. Peel pears, remove cores and cut in quarters.
2. In a small skillet over medium heat, melt the butter. Add the brown sugar and cinnamon and stir well. Add the pears and sauté until pears are slightly soft, about 1–2 minutes per side.
3. Pour the rum into the pan, heat for 1 minute and then ignite with a long match. When flames burn out, place pear quarters in two serving dishes, top with vanilla ice cream and sauce from the bottom of the pan.

Variation: Try this dish the traditional way with 2 bananas that have been cut in half the long way or 2–3 peeled, sliced peaches.

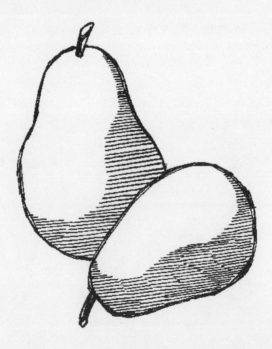

7

Moody Monday

"Love comforteth like sunshine after rain."
— *William Shakespeare*

*T*he morning paper is soaked and so are you. You start your car, already late. The highway's flooded, nothing moves. Finally, after a slow polka through the mud, you arrive at the office. No space in the company garage and no street parking. You pull into a lot, pay up and shut up: $5.00 for the first half hour and $2.50 per for the rest of the day.

It's 10:05 a.m. when you slink through the door. The boss is right there to greet you: "Nice of you to join us today, Jones," she says wondering where the report that you promised her on Friday is. The stack of messages on your desk resembles Mt. Kilimanjaro. Getting through them feels like climbing Mt. Everest. You forget your appointment book and can't remember when you're meeting with the new vice president from Finco. No coffee and the only thing in the cafeteria is wilted spinach salad left over from Friday.

At 2 p.m. you feel a tickle in the back of your throat. By 3 your eyes feel itchy and sore. By 4 you feel a little warm and your nose starts to drip like a broken faucet. By the time you get home, you need a compassionate lover, a hot bath and comfort food. Leave your *%$#^@ day at the door. Three hours to bedtime. You can still rekindle your soul while you beat back another cold. Draw a bath and dissolve your troubles in bubbles. Put on your jammies. Moan in your lover's arms. Tonight you get to be a seven-year-old again.

Now the fun part. Add comfort food to the comforting: chicken soup (because colds always start on moody Mondays), macaroni & cheese, mashed potatoes, peanut butter right from the jar, vanilla ice cream smothered in hot fudge, chocolate pudding. Snuggle under an old comforter together, rent cartoons and sip, slurp, eat or spill as much as you want. With proper comforting, you may face Tuesday with a smile or at least without a stuffed nose.

When it comes to fighting colds, we'll take chicken soup with a vitamin C chaser over Contact any day. Chicken soup is culinary penicillin that transports us back to our roots. Ten out of ten Jewish mothers we surveyed recommend chicken soup for colds. Chicken soup has been prescribed for colds since the Jewish philosopher and physician Moses Maimonides (1135–1204 A.D.) got a horrible head cold after visiting Jerusalem in the rain without his umbrella. Scientists aren't sure why chicken soup works, but studies have proven it helps fight colds and congestion. Both Mount Sinai Medical Center and the Mayo Clinic advocate using it to fight colds and congestion. We know the steam opens your sinuses, the broth soothes your throat and the love that goes into making it warms your soul.

Chicken soup is simple, basic food. Just sauté an onion, throw in a chopped carrot or some celery, add a couple cans of chicken broth and bring to a simmer. (Occasionally we make stock from scratch, but it's a lot more

FOOD & MOOD

If you've ever craved Peking ravioli, chocolate ice cream or pepperoni pizza, you probably know that mood influences food choices. But did you know that what you eat can also influence your mood?

The chemical messengers called neurotransmitters (including serotonin, dopamine, norepinephrine and acetycholine) that modulate mood and behavior are made from food. So, while a balanced diet, which provides the proper nutrients to manufacture neurotransmitters, can help prevent mood swings and keep you energized, skipping meals or consuming too much junk food, caffeine or sugar can bring you down.

---

work than opening a can of College Inn. Certainly more effort than we're up for on a Monday.) When the broth starts to simmer, you can also toss in a handful of egg noodles, cooked, chopped chicken (a great way to use leftover chicken) and 1 teaspoon dried herbs. The soup is ready when the vegetables and noodles, if you decided to use them, are soft but not mushy (this usually takes about 8–10 minutes). For knaydlakh (matza dumplings) like Grandma used to make, try Manischewitz Matza Ball Soup Mix.

Don't have a cold? Not in the mood for soup? Skip it. The key component of comfort food is you get to eat exactly and only what you want. You don't even have to finish your okra. Macaroni & cheese may be your ultimate comfort food. When was the last time you had some good old, neon orange, chemically-incorrect Kraft Macaroni & Cheese? Remember threading the pasta onto the prongs of your fork when you were a kid? The Quickie Mart is probably open and will definitely have a box. Personally we prefer our upscale Macaroni & Cheesecake to Kraft. Once you've tried our smoked gouda blend, you'll know why.

Not salivating yet? Okay, maybe you're craving mashed potatoes. Forget instant flakes. Peel, cube and boil a couple of spuds (3–4 should do it) for approximately 20 minutes. When the potatoes are tender (pierce with a fork, if the fork slides easily through them, they're done) mash them and spike with roast garlic if you like. Garlic contains natural antibiotics that can help wipe out the virus that's lurking in your throat before it turns into a full-blown cold. Add ½ cup milk or light cream to the mashed potatoes and as much butter as you like. Stir to combine, put in a casserole dish and top with 3–4 tablespoons grated cheese. Set the dish under the broiler and cook potatoes until cheese is melted and starting to brown, about 3–4 minutes.

Don't feel like cooking? Sneak up to the bedroom with your lover and

FUELING UP & CALMING DOWN

To keep yourself well charged, have a good breakfast and eat small, frequent meals throughout the day. Go easy on caffeine, sugar and fat. (Too much fat can effect neurotransmitter production.) And make sure to drink enough water, at least eight glasses a day. (Dehydration makes you feel tired and spacy.)

To increase your energy and feel more alert, try eating a high-protein meal. Protein breaks down into amino acids including tyrosine, an amino acid used to make stimulating neurotransmitters called catecholamines. To help you relax, try a carbohydrate-rich meal. Eating carbohydrates increases brain levels of serotonin, a neurotransmitter that makes you feel calmer.

feed each other gobs of peanut butter. Forget spoons, use your fingers. Buy a pint of real vanilla ice cream and crawl into bed with some hot fudge sauce. Need something warm and creamy? Make chocolate pudding. You may like this comfort food ritual so much that it becomes a regular Monday night activity.

GREAT WALL JEWISH CHICKEN SOUP

The cure-all soup integrates the healing powers of chicken soup with the wisdom of the Orient.

2 tablespoons vegetable oil

1 onion, cut in half and then cut into 1-inch thick slices

1 tablespoon fresh gingerroot, peeled and minced

4 garlic cloves, minced

1 medium carrot, cut into match sticks

1 celery stalk, cut into match sticks

1 chicken breast half, julienned

6 cups chicken broth

2 tablespoons soy sauce

1 tablespoon dark sesame oil

2 tablespoons red wine vinegar

¼ teaspoon white pepper

2 tablespoons cornstarch, dissolved in 3 tablespoons water

Dash of Tabasco sauce

1 egg, lightly beaten

¼ cup fresh parsley or cilantro, chopped

1. Heat the oil in a stockpot over medium heat. Add the onion and cook until soft, about 5 minutes. Add the gingerroot, garlic, carrot, celery and chicken. If pan gets dry add a few tablespoons chicken broth. Cook, stirring frequently, until chicken turns white, about 4 minutes.

2. Stir in the broth and bring to a simmer. Add the soy sauce, sesame oil, vinegar and white pepper and bring back to a simmer. Add the cornstarch-water mixture and Tabasco sauce. Stir until soup thickens slightly.

3. Turn off the burner, add the beaten egg in a thin stream and gently stir. Ladle soup into bowls, and garnish with parsley or cilantro.

Variations:
- Ladle soup over cooked ramen noodles.
- Skip the chicken and add a few cooked shrimp to the finished soup.

MACARONI & CHEESECAKE

It's so good we taste test it at least every other week.

1½ cups macaroni
¼ cup plus 1 tablespoon bread crumbs
1 egg
⅔ cup evaporated milk
1 teaspoon champagne mustard
⅛ teaspoon paprika
⅛ teaspoon ground white pepper
8 ounces smoked gouda, grated
2 tablespoons Parmesan cheese, grated
1 tablespoon butter, melted

1. Boil water and cook the macaroni until al dente. Drain, rinse with cold water and set aside.

2. Preheat oven to 350°F. Grease a 6-inch springform pan. Sprinkle pan with 1 tablespoon bread crumbs and shake out the excess.

3. In a small bowl beat together the egg, evaporated milk, mustard, paprika and pepper. Mix in macaroni and grated gouda cheese. Spoon mixture into prepared pan.

4. Mix together remaining bread crumbs, Parmesan cheese and melted butter. Sprinkle mixture on top of macaroni. Bake until golden brown, about 45 minutes. Let cool for about 15 minutes, remove sides of pan and serve.

MOODY MONDAY MASHERS

Dig out your mother's old hand masher and get ready for the world's best mashed potatoes.

4 baking potatoes, about 2 pounds
1 tablespoon salt
4 tablespoons butter, cut into small pieces *("Come on, Ellen, tell them*
   to use a whole stick.")
½–¾ cup milk, warmed
Salt and freshly ground black pepper, to taste.

1. Peel the potatoes and cut into 1 to 2-inch chunks.
2. Place the potatoes in a large pot and cover with cold water. Add 1 tablespoon salt. Bring water to a boil and cook until potatoes are tender, about 20 minutes. Drain the potatoes and return to the pan.
3. Using a potato masher, fork, food mill, ricer, whisk or hand mixer, coarsely mash the potatoes with the butter. (See, you can make these even if you didn't inherit a masher.)
4. Continue to mash the potatoes gradually adding enough milk or cream until they reach the "right" consistency. (Older potatoes generally need more liquid.) Make sure to find out if your date likes potatoes lumpy or creamy, thick or thin.
5. Season with salt and pepper. Sneak up to the bedroom and enjoy.

Variations:
- **Garlic.** Peel the thick outer skin off 5 garlic cloves. Boil the cloves in water until soft, about 15–20 minutes. (You can boil them with the potatoes.) Take the skin off the garlic cloves. Mash the cloves and add to the mashed potatoes.
- **Cheese.** Add 2–3 ounces grated cheese to your potatoes when you mash them or sprinkle a few tablespoons cheese on top of the potatoes and place the dish under the broiler for a few minutes to melt the cheese before serving.
- **Onion Bacon Cheddar.** Add ½ cup sautéed, chopped onion, ¼ cup crisp, cooked bacon and ¼ cup shredded cheddar cheese to the mashed potatoes before serving.

CHOCOLATE PUDDING

The ultimate comfort food.

¼ cup sugar
3 tablespoons cornstarch
¼ teaspoon salt
2 cups milk
3 ounces semisweet chocolate chips (½ cup)
1 teaspoon vanilla

1. In a large glass bowl, combine the sugar, cornstarch and salt. Pour in the milk and stir until well combined. Add the chocolate chips.
2. Microwave uncovered on high for 2 minutes. Stop and stir. Microwave for another 2 minutes. Stop and stir. Continue to microwave on high until chocolate chips are almost completely melted and pudding is thick, another 2–3 additional minutes. Stir well until chips are completely melted.
3. Add the vanilla. Cover and chill until ready to serve.

Variations:
❧ **Vanilla Pudding.** We can't imagine why you'd prefer vanilla pudding over chocolate, but if you're in the mood for America's number one flavor, omit the chocolate chips.
❧ **Mocha Pudding.** Add 1 teaspoon instant espresso powder in step 1.

FUDGE SAUCE

Enjoy this sauce over ice cream or use it for our Easy Chocolate Truffles recipe.

6 ounces semisweet chocolate chips (1 cup)
½ cup light cream
½ cup sugar
¼ teaspoon vanilla

1. Combine the chocolate, cream and sugar in a 1–2 quart saucepan. Bring to a boil. Lower heat and simmer uncovered, stirring frequently, until the sauce is smooth, about 2 minutes. Take off the heat and mix in the vanilla.
2. Serve immediately or pour into a glass jar and store in the refrigerator until ready to use. Sauce will keep for about 3 weeks. Sauce can be reheated by microwaving on high for 1–2 minutes or warming in a small saucepan.

8

Coffee, Tea or…

"Coffee should be black as the Devil, hot as Hell, pure as an angel and sweet as love."

— *Count Maurice De Talleyrand-Perigord*

*W*hen was the last time you had breakfast in bed? If you can't remember and your morning mantra is, "No time, gotta go," it's time to wake up and smell the coffee. Aren't you tired of chewing on Styrofoam cups, stamped with a clown's face and spilling bitter sludge all over yourself at every pothole? Take twenty minutes to have a muffin with your honey bunch and the whole day will look brighter.

The basis for breakfast is a good cup of coffee (this means NO instant). Start with cold water, preferably with a low mineral content. If you're not sure of your water's status, use spring or filtered water. For outstanding java measure the beans — NEVER GUESS. How strong to brew the coffee depends on your taste. In general, 2 tablespoons (1 coffee scoop) to 6 ounces water makes a medium-strength cup. Use whole beans, preferably ground right before brewing. The best coffee is made with freshly roasted beans, so buy beans in small batches from a roaster or a market with a quick turnover. To avoid bitter coffee, don't over grind the beans. For drip or press (Melior) coffee makers, grind for about 10 seconds. Store coffee in the freezer in airtight tins. It will keep fresh for several weeks.

Coffee, like wine, varies in terms of flavor, body, aroma and acidity. Taste depends on where the coffee originated, when it was picked and how it was roasted. The two main types of coffee plants are Arabica and Robusta. Arabica coffee is grown slowly at high altitudes, contains less caffeine and has a superior, complex flavor. Robusta coffee, which is generally used for blends and instant, is much hardier and easier to grow but lacks flavor.

Sampling coffee (called cupping) is similar to wine tasting and a lot of fun. After brewing a cup, smell its aroma. Is it spicy? Does it suggest flowers or chocolate? (Hawaiian Kona and good Colombians have a clean, floral smell.) Next close your eyes and sip. Note if the flavor is rich, complex or balanced. Does it have a bitter or acid (tart) aftertaste? (Kenya AA has a strong acid note similar to a dry wine.) Finally take a swig and swirl the brew around in your mouth. You should be able to tell if it is a light or full-bodied coffee.

If you don't own a coffee maker, get one. Most appliance or general merchandise stores have a wide variety of choices, and nowadays they're pretty inexpensive. You can get a good-quality unit for as little as $25.00. Make sure your coffee maker is clean. You won't impress anyone if you start the day with yesterday's grounds.

We prefer a drip-filter system because it's easy, always makes a good cup and keeps the coffee warm in case the mood hits and we decide to get back in bed. For a few dollars more you can buy a machine with an automatic timer so that your coffee will be waiting with the morning paper. (With our paperboy the coffee always arrives first.) The first night in our new house we couldn't find the alarm clock among the boxes, so we set the coffee maker up in our bedroom and woke right on time to the perk-perk-perk of French roast.

Recently we bought a bread machine to keep the coffee maker company. On some mornings we wake to the smell of a freshly baked loaf which harmonizes beautifully with morning lovemaking. There's nothing better than being greeted in the morning by warm, fresh-baked bread. All you need to do the night before is measure flour, yeast, salt, water and extras like honey, oatmeal, nuts or raisins. Set the timer and good night. In the morning, violà: warm, fresh bread.

You don't need a bread machine to have fresh-baked goods in the morning. Muffin, pancake or waffle batter can be prepared, refrigerated and made the next morning. Short on time? Make muffins over the weekend and stash in the freezer. Or for fresh muffins during the week pour batter into muffin tins lined with aluminum foil, cover with plastic wrap or more foil and freeze for up to two weeks. When ready to bake, remove frozen muffin batter from foil, grease the pan the muffins were frozen in, place frozen batter in tins and bake in preheated 375°F oven for 30–45 minutes. Oh, and don't forget great and glorious Jiffy Corn Muffin Mix for the best corn muffins on the planet in 15–20 minutes.

They say France's greatest achievement was the invention of romance. We say it's the croissant. Chocolate, ham and cheese, raspberry and especially almond bring out the Jean Paul Belmondo and Catherine Deneuve in us all. Can't get fresh croissants in your hamlet? Then invite the Pillsbury Dough Boy home or look in the freezer of your grocery store for frozen croissants or puff pastry to butter up and roll your own.

Skip the Wonder Bread and margarine. Take the time, have an adventure, bake a crusty, chewy, crumbly, sweet, savory or succulent loaf or batch for tomorrow morning. You may discover that man and woman can live on bread alone when it's buttered with love.

WHAT TO BREW

Legend has it that coffee was discovered by a Turkish shepherd in the 9th century who observed that his goats became rather perky and began zipping around the pasture after munching on beans from a certain bush. In the 13th century these energizing beans were roasted and coffee was born. Today, coffee, which grows from the Tropic of Cancer to the Tropic of Capricorn, is the largest-traded food commodity on the planet.

Several factors determine a coffee's character: place of origin, whether the coffee is a blend or a single bean and type of roast. Here's a summary to help you pick your beans.

Place of Origin
Central and South America
Coffees from this region are usually bright, mild, light-to-medium bodied and balanced.

East Africa and Arabia
Coffees from this region tend to be snappy, exotic, intense; and medium-to-full bodied.

Indonesia and the Pacific
Coffees from this region are usually smooth, full-bodied, low in acidity and earthy.

Here are some of our favorite single-origin beans:
• Sumatra. A heavier-bodied coffee with a long finish from the East Indies.
• Guatemalan Antigua. A lively, luscious cup hailed for its dark chocolate, spicy flavor.

• Mexican Altura. Its mellow, gentle flavor and light-body makes it the perfect breakfast brew.
• Colombian Supremo. A nicely balanced coffee from Latin America.
• Brazil Especial. A delicate, sweet, gentle coffee with a surprisingly hearty aftertaste.
• Kenya AA. A strong, full-bodied coffee with a rich, fruity flavor. One of the best quality coffees available.

Blends
Blends are mixtures of different types of coffees and tend to be more consistent, balanced and complex than most single bean coffees. The flavor of the blend depends on what characteristics the coffee roaster wants.

Roasts
The roasting process burns off some of the acidic flavor and leaves a smoother, mellower cup with less caffeine.
• Light City or Pale. Roasted for the least amount of time, they have a delicate, acidic flavor.
• American or Full City. The most common roasts; roasted longer than Light City.
• French and Viennese. These roasts produce a darker, richer coffee.
• Italian or Espresso. These are the darkest roasts and have a rich, bittersweet edge like Robert Di Niro on a good day. Savor a cup with biscotti.

CHOCOLATE CHIP BREAD

The chocolate chip version of this bread was inspired by a visit to Club Med where the decadence never ends and chocolate is always available.

> 1 order pizza dough, about 1 pound*
> 1 tablespoon butter, melted, plus additional butter for brushing
> dough before baking
> 1 cup semisweet chocolate chips

1. Grease a cookie sheet. Stretch the pizza dough on a floured surface into a rectangle that measures approximately 15 x 10-inches.

2. Brush one side of the dough with 1 tablespoon melted butter. Sprinkle the dough with chocolate chips.

3. Roll dough up starting at the long side. Pinch seam to seal dough. Place on greased cookie sheet, seam side down, and brush top with additional butter.

4. Cover dough with plastic wrap and a clean dish towel and let rise in a warm place for about 30–45 minutes.

5. Preheat oven to 350°F. Cut a few slits, about 1-inch deep, in the top of the bread to let steam escape during baking. Bake until bread is golden brown and sounds hollow when you tap it, about 30 minutes.

Variation: Cardamom Cocoa Cinnamon Bread. Substitute the following mixture for the chocolate chips in step 2: ¼ cup cocoa, ½ cup sugar, 1 teaspoon cinnamon, 1½ teaspoon cardamom, †½ cup coarsely chopped walnuts, ½ cup raisins.

* *Raw pizza dough is available at many pizzerias and also in the refrigerator or freezer sections of grocery stores.*
† *Cardamom is believed to promote love and lust, so sprinkle plenty of it around.*

GINGER PEAR MUFFINS

Tired of blueberry and bran muffins? Pop some of these in the oven for a new twist on an old favorite.

1¾ cup flour
2 teaspoons baking powder
½ teaspoon baking soda
1 teaspoon powdered ginger
½ teaspoon cinnamon
Pinch of salt
½ cup butter
¾ cup sugar
2 eggs, lightly beaten
¼ cup milk
1 teaspoon vanilla
¼ cup candied ginger, chopped
4 canned pear halves, chopped

1. Preheat oven to 350°F. Grease muffin tins.
2. Sift the flour, baking powder, baking soda, powdered ginger, cinnamon and salt into a medium-size bowl and set aside.
3. Cream together the butter and sugar until light, fluffy and lemon colored. Add the eggs, one at a time, beating well after each addition. Add the milk and vanilla and stir well to combine.
4. Add the flour mixture and stir until just combined.
5. Fold in the pears and candied ginger.
6. Pour into the greased muffin tins, filling two-thirds of the way. Bake in preheated oven until muffins are golden brown, about 25–30 minutes.

Variations: Substitute the following ingredients for the powdered and candied ginger, cinnamon and pears.

❧ **Banana Chocolate Chip.** Fold in 1 chopped banana and ½ cup chocolate chips.
❧ **Blueberry.** Fold in 1 cup fresh or frozen blueberries.

CINNAMON BUNS

The aroma is guaranteed to get your partner's attention.

3 tablespoons butter or margarine, melted
¼ cup brown sugar
2 tablespoons honey
1 teaspoon cinnamon
1 teaspoon vanilla
⅓ cup pecans, coarsely chopped
⅓ cup raisins
1 package of 12 refrigerator biscuits

1. Preheat the oven to 425°F. Grease an 8 or 9-inch round baking dish.

2. Combine the melted butter, brown sugar, honey, cinnamon, vanilla, chopped pecans and raisins. Spread the mixture in the prepared dish. Place biscuits on top of the butter mixture.

3. Bake until buns are golden brown, about 8–12 minutes. To serve, invert dish onto plate and let buns slide out so that the cinnamon nut mixture is on top.

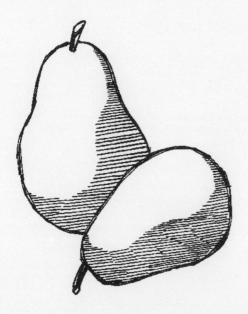

PEANUT BUTTER BISCOTTI

Perfect for morning dunking or partnered with Sloshed Slush for dessert. These freeze well, so make extra.

    2¾ cups flour
    1¾ cups sugar
    1 teaspoon baking powder
    ½ teaspoon salt
    3 eggs, beaten
    ⅓ cup peanut butter
    ¼ cup water
    1¼ cups unsalted, roasted peanuts

1. Preheat oven to 350°F. Grease a cookie sheet.
2. In a large bowl mix the flour, sugar, baking powder and salt.
3. In a separate bowl, lightly beat together the eggs, peanut butter and water. Add to flour mixture and mix just until ingredients are incorporated. A little more water, a teaspoon at a time, can be added if mixture is too dry to make a smooth dough. Stir in the peanuts.
4. Divide the dough into two portions, and form each into a log approximately 3-inches in diameter. Place the logs on prepared cookie sheet about 3–4 inches apart. Flatten logs slightly with your palm. Bake in pre-heated oven until light brown, about 40 minutes. Take out of the oven.
5. Turn the oven down to 300°F. Let logs cool for 10 minutes and then cut into ¾-inch thick bars. Place bars, cut side down, back on the baking sheet, and cook until biscotti are crisp, about 20 minutes.

HAM & CHEESE CROISSANTS

A French classic that's perfect for breakfast in bed.

    1 package of 6 refrigerator croissant rolls
    ¼ pound boiled Danish ham
    ¼ pound Swiss cheese, sliced

1. Preheat oven to 350°F. Lightly grease a cookie sheet.
2. Unroll croissants. Lay a piece of cheese and a piece of ham across each roll. Roll up dough and place on greased cookie sheet. Repeat for remaining rolls.
3. Bake until golden brown, about 8–10 minutes.

9

Honey Bee Mine

Honey 1. a sweet, viscid material elaborated out of the nectar of flowers in the honey sack of various bees. 2. sweetheart, dear.

—*Webster's Dictionary*

*W*ant to get stung by Cupid? Then you have to sweeten the pot with a drop of honey to woo your love.

Honey, as old as the pyramids and sweeter than an angel's kiss, has been lubricating the gears of love from the beginning of recorded time. Bees are one of the oldest forms of life on the planet. They've been buzzing around for at least 10 million years. The busy creatures laid the foundation for our "sweet tooth," and we've spent centuries trying to fill it.

While modern humans crave sugar, ancient cultures revered honey. Cavemen loved the sticky stuff and left rock paintings depicting their quests for honey. Before sugar became available, sweets made with honey were a luxury only the wealthy could afford.

An Egyptian probably invented the first candy: a gooey mess of seeds, nuts, dried fruit and spices glued together with a bit of honey. The Egyptians believed honey had magical powers; they offered honey to their gods and used it for medicine. Aristotle called honey, "dew distilled from the stars and the rainbow," and for centuries the Greeks ate honey to remain youthful. Pharaohs were buried with honey, and parts of Alexander the Great were buried in honey.

> *"Which parts?"*
> *"Stop it, Ellen."*
> *"I want to know."*
> *"I'll tell you later."*

Today, the magic of honey survives in our language. Honey, the symbol of love and wisdom, is believed to protect newlyweds. Honeymoon refers to the

---

BUSY AS A BEE

Honey is made by bees who gather nectar, usually from flowers, in their honey sacks and turn it into honey. Bees have been known to turn everything from cola to cotton candy into honey. Bees accomplish this alchemy through the application of specific enzymes found in their saliva and gastric juices. After a long day out in the fields, the bees return to the hive, regurgitate the nectar and deposit it in the honeycomb.

Worker bees then concentrate the stockpiled nectar turning it into honey. The process is extremely labor intensive. To produce one pound of honey, a colony of bees collectively travels about 75,000 miles. (If anybody ever needed a union, it's these guys.) Each hive must make eight pounds of honey to yield one pound for human consumption.

GIFT OF THE GODS

The Egyptians offered honey to the god of fertility, Min. If you ever saw any of this guy's statues you would know why he got the job. He is often pictured with a very proud, and we mean VERY PROUD, erection.

Many ancient religions considered honey divine. According to one Greek myth, Zeus was born in a cave guarded by bees who cared for him.

The Mayan Indians believed that the bee was born at the center of the earth and was sent to keep man from indifference and ignorance.

One Egyptian legend recalls that the god Ra cried and his tears became bees that produced honey.

---

old European custom where newlyweds drank mead (honey wine) during their first lunar month together. Indians serve milk and honey at weddings. Hindu priests, notorious spoil sports, abstained from honey because of its reputation as an aphrodisiac.

Mead, which is brewed from honey, was probably the first alcoholic beverage. Ancient Egyptians, Greeks and Romans diluted honey with water and let it ferment. The result was a potent, intoxicating brew perfect for their saturnalian orgies. The Inca and Aztec Indians, not to be out done by the ancients, also brewed mead. We suggest you try it yourself. We do our part by brewing anniversary mead each year and drinking the previous year's batch on our anniversary to celebrate our marriage.

Honey is one of the few foods made by insects that humans eat and the only food that does not seem to spoil. Jars of honey found in ancient tombs are still edible. Honey does crystallize however. If you reach for a jar and it's gotten chunky, set it in a pan of water and heat gently or warm it up in a microwave oven for a few minutes. To keep your honey happy, store in a covered jar at room temperature.

In addition to being sweet and spreadable, honey can also be substituted for sugar. Baked goods made with honey are chewier and stay moist longer than those sweetened with sugar. You can substitute honey for up to half the sugar in a recipe. Honey is sweeter than sugar so when substituting honey in recipes, use about ⅞ of a cup of honey for each cup of sugar. For each cup of honey used, cut back the liquid ingredients in your recipe by ¼ cup, and add an additional ½ teaspoon baking powder for baked goods.

If you have all afternoon, you can attempt baklava or halava, but it's WORK and The Cooking Couple don't cook nothin' if the work gets in the way of the fun. Let's face it, there are better ways to play with honey than baking baklava. Drizzle it on bread, toast, corn muffins, biscuits, pancakes, berries or...

31 FLAVORS?

When you think of honey, you don't generally think about flavors, but there is one to fit every taste, from strong, dark buckwheat to delicate clover. You may want to try thyme, orange blossom, rosemary, sage or heather. Use mildly flavored honeys, like clover, for delicately flavored dishes such as our Honey Mustard Chicken. Use strong honeys, like buckwheat, when you want a dish to have a distinct honey flavor as in spreads or sauces.

HONEY MUSTARD CHICKEN

Can't decide what to make for dinner? Short on time and patience? This chicken recipe takes less than 5 minutes to prepare before baking.

> 2 tablespoons butter or margarine
> 3 tablespoons honey
> 3 tablespoons Dijon mustard
> ½ teaspoon dried thyme
> Salt and freshly ground black pepper, to taste
> 1 chicken, cut into pieces

1. Preheat oven to 375°F. Cover a large baking pan, big enough to hold the chicken pieces, with aluminum foil.
2. Melt the butter or margarine. Combine melted butter or margarine with the honey, mustard, thyme, salt and pepper.
3. Place the chicken in the prepared pan. Brush the honey mustard mixture on the chicken.
4. Bake until the chicken is cooked through, about 45 minutes.

Variation: Aromatic Chinese Chicken. Combine the honey with 2 tablespoons vegetable oil, 2 tablespoons soy sauce, 2 tablespoons sherry, 1 teaspoon five-spice powder and 2 chopped scallions. Cook as above. If possible marinate the chicken in the mixture for several hours before cooking.

WHITE CHOCOLATE HONEY MOUSSE

Easy, elegant and extremely rich. Great after a light supper.

6 ounces white chocolate, chopped
2 tablespoons honey
1½ cups chilled whipping cream
1 (1 ounce) dark chocolate bar, optional

1. Place the white chocolate in a glass container and microwave on medium for 2–3 minutes, stopping to stir after about 1 minute. Chocolate can also be melted in the top of a double boiler placed about 1-inch away from simmering (not boiling) water.

2. Take chocolate off heat. Stir in the honey and ½ cup whipping cream. Let cool to room temperature.

3. When the chocolate mixture has cooled, whip remaining cream until it forms soft peaks. Gently fold the cream into the chocolate mixture. Pour the mixture into four wine glasses, cover and set in refrigerator for at least two hours. Garnish with shaved dark chocolate if desired. To shave chocolate let the chocolate bar come to room temperature and shave using a sharp carrot peeler.

HONEY FRENCH TOAST

A delicious way to start the day.

½ cup milk
¼ cup honey
½ teaspoon vanilla
2 eggs, beaten
8 slices challah or Italian bread, preferably slightly stale

1. Heat a griddle or fry pan. Combine the milk, honey, vanilla and beaten eggs.

2. Butter griddle with about 1–2 teaspoons butter or margarine. Dip bread into egg mixture and fry each side until golden brown. Serve with cinnamon sugar or one of the following sauces or butters.

HONEY LEMON SAUCE

Spread this sauce on toast or muffins.

1 tablespoon melted butter
½ cup honey
1 tablespoon lemon juice

1. Combine the melted butter, honey and lemon juice and mix until smooth.

HALAVA SAUCE

Try this sauce with fresh fruit.

1 cup plain yogurt
2 tablespoons sesame tahini
2–3 tablespoons honey (depending on how sweet you want it)

1. Combine all ingredients and mix until smooth.

HONEY BERRY SAUCE

Serve this sauce over ice cream.

3 cups frozen berries
¼ cup honey
¾ cup apple juice

1. Allow berries to thaw. Drain berries reserving ½ cup liquid.
2. Combine reserved liquid, honey and apple juice in a small saucepan over high heat. Bring to a boil. Reduce heat and simmer until liquid is reduced to about 1 cup. Let cool.
3. Stir in berries.

HONEY BUTTER

Spread on your favorite baked goods.

4 tablespoons butter, allowed to come to room temperature
¼ cup honey

1. Mix the butter with the honey until smooth.

Variations:
- **Honey Citrus Butter.** Add ½ teaspoon grated lemon or orange peel.
- **Hot Honey Butter.** Add a dash of Tabasco sauce or cayenne pepper and serve with rolls, corn bread or biscuits.

10

Just Desserts

"A gourmet who thinks of calories is like a
tart who looks at her watch."

—*James Beard*

*W*e said there are no desserts in this book because you are dessert. Okay, we lied. Even a dish like you can use a little whipped cream. Besides, how could we write a romantic cookbook without singing the praises of chocolate? Truth be told: Desserts are a whole mouth watering arena all their own. We couldn't live without them. (Actually, Ellen couldn't live without them. Michael couldn't live without chicken wings.) Desserts let us go wild, be bad and use plenty of butter. So, parade your sweet tooth, indulge, let yourself go, be sinful and show off.

Don't panic. You won't need to run out to Kitchen Etc. to purchase a special set of Martha Stewart autographed bake ware with a three-speed etiquette mixer to concoct our creations. These dessert recipes, like most of the other recipes in our book, are fun and easy.

Although we love cannoli and triple chocolate layer cake, we have no business making these delectable treats. Leave the triple layer cake with the mocha butter cream frosting to the master baker with a culinary degree who gets up at 4:00 a.m. to make sure the sweets are ready for you. Buy the cake, embellish with ice cream, get in bed and enjoy.

Desserts can be light, fruity palate cleansers (try our recipe for Sloshed Slush); sumptuous, dark and wicked; or creamy, smooth and tender. While salads and steaks feed the body, desserts feed the soul. Whether you're sharing apple pie à la mode or chocolate fondue, dessert turns a meal into an event. Perfect for sharing and great in bed, desserts are like a lover who never complains and always entertains.

> *"I thought I was great in bed."*
> *"You are, Michael."*
> *"So what do you need desserts for?"*
> *"Desserts never fall asleep."*

The craving for sweets is programmed into our souls just like our desire for love and cuddling. Humans are drawn to sweets from birth and for good reason. Sweet foods are filled with calories. (Babies are born with extra taste buds in their cheeks specifically for sweets. That's why breast milk is warm and sweet.) Yes, there was a time long ago and far away when calories were not enemies. For thousands of years famine lurked around the corner, and people actually needed surplus calories to survive. Now, with the abundance of food and lack of exercise in the Western world, we fight calories to stay thin.

In moderation sweets are good for you. They play a role in controlling moods and can relieve a crank attack, especially when combined with fat and chocolate. The carbohydrates in sweets (usually sugar) raise the brain's level

A SHORT, SWEET, HISTORY OF CHOCOLATE

The Aztecs were the first chocoholics. They ground cocoa beans, added spices and drank the bitter brew without sugar.

In 1519, the Spanish explorer Cortez was the first European to taste chocolate. Montezuma, the Aztec king, thinking Cortez was a god, offered the explorer the Aztec's greatest treasure — heaps of cocoa beans. The Spaniards introduced chocolate to Europe where it was mixed with sugar and quickly became popular, despite attempts by the clergy to abolish chocolate by claiming it was connected to the "heathen" practices of the Aztecs.

Initially sipping cocoa was a highly taxed luxury in Europe, enjoyed only by the very wealthy. Eventually the brew trickled down to the masses. In 1657 the first chocolate tavern opened in London. Drinking hot cocoa became chic among Brits, and chocolate developed a reputation as an aphrodisiac.

Toward the end of the 17th century, a Frenchman named David Chaillon discovered how to evaporate the liquid in chocolate and mold it into solid shapes. He was appointed Royal Chocolate Maker to the King by Louis XIV and enjoyed a 23-year monopoly on French chocolate sales.

In the 18th century, chocolate plants sprang up across Europe. The Austrians were the first to bake chocolate cakes, and the Swiss invented milk chocolate, America's favorite chocolate, in 1875.

In 1765, Dr. James Baker, father of Baker's Chocolate, opened the first American chocolate plant. The good doctor marketed chocolate as a restorative for many ailments, including impotency. One-hundred years later in San Francisco, Domingo Ghirardelli started making ground chocolate. Twenty-nine years later, Milton Hershey invented the Hershey Bar. In 1930, Ruth Wakefield, hostess at the Toll House Inn, added a cut-up bar of semisweet chocolate to a batch of cookie dough and invented the chocolate chip cookie. She promptly informed Nestle of her discovery, who responded by printing her recipe on the back of its chocolate bar. Nine years later, Nestle started making chocolate chips.

of serotonin (a neurotransmitter that influences mood and creates a sense of well-being). Sweet foods also generate a rush of endorphins (the body's natural pain killers), making us feel tranquil and calm. The fat, often present in sweets, appeases a primitive desire for calories. And while chocolate is no substitute for love, the heady food can make you feel good. Chocolate contains over 400 substances including phenylethylamine (PEA), a brain chemical that some scientists believe arouses the feelings we experience when we are in love, as well as the stimulants caffeine and theobromine. And

HOT! HOT! HOT! CHOCOLATE

Cocoa cotillions were a big hit among the Aztecs. One ritual, celebrating the chocolate harvest, ended with the presentation of 2,000 cups of cocoa served in gold goblets by naked virgins to the emperor and his court.

Montezuma, reported to be a virile lover, never entertained his harem without first taking a swig of cocoa.

The first cocoa contained chilies and musk and took some getting used to. We think you'll prefer our recipe for Mexican chocolate.

3 squares unsweetened chocolate (3 ounces)
2 cups milk
1/3 cup sugar
1/8 teaspoon nutmeg
1/8 teaspoon cinnamon
1 egg white (optional)

1. Heat the milk and chocolate just below a boil and cook until the chocolate is melted.
2. Add the sugar, nutmeg and cinnamon. Beat with a molinillo (a special wooden chocolate beater) or a whisk until foamy.
3. Either serve immediately or whip an egg white until foamy; gently fold into the chocolate and serve.

---

although chocolate is rich and fattening, new studies suggest that the saturated fat in chocolate (mostly stearic acid) doesn't raise "bad" LDL cholesterol or lower "good" HDL cholesterol. So the next time your lover is blue, lethargic or testy, give your mate a Hershey's kiss.

Women crave sweet foods (especially during PMS when serotonin levels dip) and fats. According to the publication *Appetite*, chocolate candy is the number-one food craved by women followed by ice cream; cakes, cookies and pastry; fruit and Chinese food. Men frequently crave foods high in protein and fat. The generalization holds true in our household. When Michael gets a craving it's usually for steak, chicken wings or pizza. Dessert is an afterthought easily filled by a handful of raisins. Ellen contemplates the dessert menu before considering what to have for dinner. If there's no dessert worthy of her palate, she insists on stopping for ice cream.

> *"Stop the chapter, I need something sweet NOW!"*
>
> *"If it's this bad now, I can't wait to see what it's like when you're pregnant."*
>
> *"Stop joking."*
>
> *"You had something sweet this morning."*

"That was you, now I want chocolate."
"I saw you snitch some sweets less than two paragraphs ago."
"I don't care. STOP NOW."

Wow, that's why I always keep chocolate hidden around the house. When Ellen gets cranky I head for the "Use only in emergency" Hershey's kisses. Notice how Ellen isn't saying anything for a change? She's munching through the sweets drawer in the kitchen. How else do you think I could say this much without her butting in?

Without chocolate, Halloween candy would consist of gum, jelly beans and candy corn. There would be no hot cocoa, Reese's peanut butter cups, fudge, devil's food cake or Godiva. The average American eats approximately 11.2 pounds of chocolate a year. For Valentine's Day couples across the country spend approximately $665 million on chocolate and other confections and buy 30 million heart-shaped boxes of candy. Traditionally women are showered with chocolate on Valentine's Day. But 48% of men aged 18–24, and 68% of men over 55 say they would rather receive chocolate than flowers.

Chocolate and cocoa come from the bitter seeds of the cocoa tree, Theobroma cacao. (Appropriately named since, Theobromais is Greek for "food of the gods.") Like coffee beans, different cocoa seeds are blended and roasted to obtain a desired flavor. The meat of the seeds (nibs) is pressed, yielding chocolate liquor that is then poured into molds where it becomes unsweetened (bitter) chocolate. The love food can then be transformed into hot fudge sundaes, chocolate frosting, chocolate chip cookies, chocolate ice cream, chocolate bars, chocolate milk, chocolate mousse and our favorite, chocolate fondue.

Chocolate burns easily so melt it slowly in a double boiler. (The top pot should be at least 1-inch from the water, not in it.) Don't let the water boil, keep it just below a simmer and don't let the chocolate get hotter than 115°F. Start with chopped chocolate — it melts faster — and don't let a drop of water mix with the chocolate. (Water makes chocolate ball-up, which keeps it from melting.) You can also melt chocolate in the microwave. Chop chocolate, place in a glass container and microwave on medium (low for milk or white chocolate), stir often and stop microwaving just before the chocolate is completely melted. Add a few tablespoons of rum, cream or coffee to your chocolate, and you have fondue perfect for dipping everything from strawberries to sticky fingers.

When it comes to chocolate, don't skimp. Buy the best quality available. Don't even think about purchasing imitation or artificial chocolate. Why waste the calories? Chocolate should be wrapped tightly and stored in a cool, dry place. Although we recommend frozen Milky Way bars, don't keep chocolate you plan to cook with in the refrigerator or freezer. When you take it out, it may sweat and not melt correctly. If stored properly, chocolate should keep for about four months. We've never tested this theory because chocolate never makes it past four days in our house.

BROWNIES

For a guaranteed second date, serve with ice cream and hot fudge sauce.

6 tablespoons unsalted butter
¾ cup sugar
12 ounces chocolate chips (2 cups)
3 eggs
1 teaspoon vanilla
¾ cup flour
¼ teaspoon baking powder
½ cup chopped nuts (optional)

1. Preheat the oven to 325°F. Grease an 8 or 9-inch square baking pan.
2. In a medium saucepan combine the butter and sugar. Set over medium heat and cook until the butter melts and mixture just starts to boil.
3. Take pan off heat, add ½ (1 cup) of the chocolate chips. Stir until chocolate is completely melted. Allow mixture to cool for a few minutes.
4. Add the vanilla and eggs, one at a time, beating well with a portable

mixer or whisk after each addition, until mixture is smooth. Using a spoon, stir in the flour and baking powder, mixing just until ingredients are well combined. Fold in the remaining cup chocolate chips and nuts.
5. Bake until toothpick inserted in the brownies comes out clean, about 30–40 minutes. Let brownies cool in pan for about 10 minutes before cutting.

Variation: Mocha Brownies. Add 1 teaspoon instant espresso powder with the first chocolate addition in step 3.

SLOSHED SLUSH

A light, refreshing dessert that will leave you giddy.

   2 cups orange juice
   1 cup sugar
   4 cups frozen strawberries, thawed
   1 bottle chilled champagne

1. In a medium saucepan gently heat orange juice and sugar until sugar dissolves. Let cool to room temperature.

2. Place the strawberries in a blender or food processor and purée.

3. Stir together the orange juice mixture, strawberry purée and champagne. Freeze the mixture in a large rectangular pan (about 13 x 9-inches), stirring every 30 minutes to 1 hour, making sure to stir crystals around edges of pan back into the liquid, until you have slush. (This takes about 3 hours.) Alternatively, freeze mixture in ice cube trays until firm and store cubes in a plastic bags. When ready to serve, place a layer of cubes in a food processor or blender and pulse on and off until chunks are gone and you have just crystals. Serve in wine glasses.

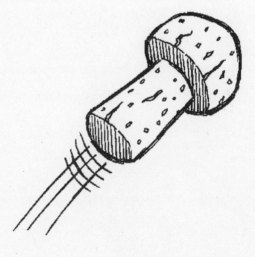

WHITE CHOCOLATE BLUEBERRY TART

The in-laws love this one.

 1 frozen puff pastry sheet (½ of a 17¼-ounce package)
 ½ cup blueberry jam
 3 tablespoons white chocolate, chopped
 1 egg, beaten with 1 tablespoon water

1. Allow the puff pastry sheet to thaw at room temperature for 20–30 minutes.
2. On a lightly floured surface, roll out the puff pastry dough to a 12 x 10 inch rectangle. With a sharp, lightly floured knife, cut the rectangle in half the long way so that you have two 12 x 5-inch sheets.
3. Place one pastry sheet on a greased baking sheet. Leaving a ¾-inch border around all four edges, spread the pastry sheet with the blueberry jam and sprinkle with white chocolate. Brush the boarders with a little beaten egg.
4. Place the remaining pastry sheet on top of the jam-covered sheet. Press the edges together to seal, and brush the entire top with beaten egg.
5. Chill the prepared tart for at least 20 minutes. (Tart can be made ahead and stored in the refrigerator for a few hours before cooking.) Preheat oven to 375°F. Bake until golden brown, about 20–30 minutes.

Variation: Cherry Chocolate Tart. Use cherry jam instead of blueberry and semisweet chocolate instead of white chocolate.

EASY CHOCOLATE TRUFFLES

You don't need a special occasion to enjoy these, just 45 minutes on the Stairmaster.

 1 cup chocolate Fudge Sauce (see page 62)
 ½ cup unsweetened cocoa

1. Chill the Fudge Sauce in the freezer for 8 hours or overnight.
2. Scoop out 1 tablespoon sauce and roll into a ball. Repeat with remaining sauce. Roll the balls in the cocoa, cover with plastic wrap, place back in the freezer and chill for another 8–10 hours.
3. Take truffles out of freezer and serve. Store remaining truffles (as if there will be any left) covered in the freezer.

11

Sexy Salads

"The truth has dawned that fresh vegetables are not only good for you, they are wonderfully good to eat — when lovingly prepared."

— *Julia Child*

Salads are more than bowls of lettuce munched through enroute to the main course. Salads can be a seductive intro, the main event, a refresher course or a side dish. Spring salads call for baby vegetables and lettuce. Summer salads rev up the appetite and keep you from wilting. Fall salads are a gardener's delight, showcasing the harvest. Warm salads are perfect in the winter when the only visible green is on a traffic light.

OIL & VINEGAR—OPPOSITES ATTRACT

The best dressed salads start with good quality oil and vinegar. Quality oils are "cold pressed." (Heat and chemicals are not used to extract the oils.) Although they don't last as long as chemically-processed oils and are pricey, they have much more flavor.

Extra virgin olive oil (a mellow, flavorful oil made only from the first pressing of special olives) is a good romantic choice. A few drops of distinctive dark sesame, rich hazelnut, subtle almond or smooth walnut oil will drive your date nuts. Try different oils to find ones you like. (Feel free to use them in our basic salad dressing recipes.)

Specialty food stores and health food stores often have a large selection of interesting oils. With oils you get what you pay for. Cheap, lackluster vegetable oils should be avoided. If you can't remember when you bought your last bottle of oil, smell the oil to make sure it isn't rancid. To help keep oils fresh, store in a cool, dark place.

There's more to vinegar than the bottle of white you bought to clean your coffee maker. Vinegars can be made from wine, cider, sherry and even champagne. They come flavored with fruit, herbs and even chili peppers. The strength of vinegars varies so adjust the ratio of oil and vinegar to your taste. Real Italian balsamic vinegar is aged in wooden barrels and has a rich, mellow flavor. Champagne vinegar is light and sweet. Red wine vinegar is a great all purpose vinegar. Rice vinegars work well in Oriental salads. Buy vinegars that have been allowed to ferment without chemicals or pasteurization. Again try your gourmet or health food store.

Forget flavorless iceberg, Kraft dressing and Bacos. Get inspired. Create a sexy, soulful, classic or exotic mix. There's more to life than cucumber rounds and tomato wedges. Virtually any ingredient can be part of your salad. Fruits, vegetables, pasta, greens, grains, chicken, beef, shellfish, herbs and spices should all be part of your salad arsenal.

Always buy the freshest ingredients available. During the summer and autumn, we buy fruits and vegetables from a local farm stand where the produce grows a few hundred yards away from the cash register. In the winter we rely more on grocery stores, canned vegetables (such as roasted red peppers, water chestnuts and artichoke hearts), frozen produce, sprouts and hearty greens like spinach. For variety, explore supermarkets, health food stores and farmers' markets. Don't be shy. Experiment and shop with your nose and eyes. Try planting a few lettuce seeds in a window box, or buy a pot of herbs to snip at your leisure.

Be careful not to overwhelm your salad with too many ingredients. Choose two or three different types of greens to start with. Light greens such as Boston, bib, red, green or oak leaf lettuce hold dressings well and form a nice platform for other ingredients. Next you can add heavier, heartier greens such as spinach, escarole or romaine. Although a little pricey, a handful of mesclun (a mix of herbs and small lettuce leaves) adds flavor, texture and color. Arugula and watercress add a peppery flavor. Sorrel, available wild or in the produce section of your supermarket, has a wonderful sour, lemony flavor and is high in vitamin C. Feeling weak, nervous or depressed? Try a leaf or two of borage. Native to North Africa and Southern Europe, borage is available between May and October in many specialty stores that sell herbs. Borage tastes a little like cucumber, is easy to grow and popular with gardeners because of its pretty star-shaped flowers, which are also edible. The herb is renowned for its ability to drive away sadness and bring courage and strength to those who eat it.

"So does Scotch."

"Michael, this is the salad chapter."

"You've never heard of Scotch dressing? Three parts Johnny Walker and one part ice."

"Please be quiet. This is my chapter."

Need a few more ideas? There's basil (believed to have mysterious restorative qualities), bitter Belgian endive, dandelion, amaranth and chives. For a shot of red, try bitter radicchio or red cabbage. If you're really adventurous, top your salad off with a few peppery nasturtium flowers, some rose petals or a handful of violets.

A ROSE BY ANY OTHER NAME NEVER TASTED SO SWEET

Many flowers are made for munching. Edible flowers (either whole buds of small flowers or petals) make beautiful garnishes and interesting additions to salads, soups and beverages.

There are a few rules to remember before chomping on a bouquet.

1. DON'T eat ANY blossom unless you are ABSOLUTELY sure it is edible (Edible Botany 101).

2. DON'T eat ANY flowers unless you know they have NOT been sprayed with pesticides. This means you can't go into a florist shop and order half-a-dozen roses for take-out. Visit your friend in Vermont with the organic garden and steal a few blossoms.

3. Flowers are fragile and wilt easily. So, pick flowers right before serving, or store loosely in a plastic bag in the refrigerator and dip the flowers in cold water before serving to revive them.

4. Sprinkle flowers on your salad AFTER tossing salad with dressing.

Wash, trim and store the greens as soon as you get home. Your greens will keep longer, and you'll be ready to prepare the salad of your life in a flash. Discard leaves with brown spots. (Actually, don't buy greens with brown spots.) Cut off the hard stem end from the heads of lettuce. This is the only time to use a knife on lettuce which should always be torn by hand (with the exception of shredded iceberg lettuce, if used immediately), not cut. When the metal blade of a knife comes in contact with lettuce, a chemical reaction occurs that turns the lettuce brown at the point of contact.

Separate the leaves with your hands. Next plunge the leaves into cold water and swirl them around to remove the dirt. Do not neglect this step, unless your date is a parakeet who will appreciate the grit. Wet greens become wilted greens; water dilutes the dressing and prevents it from sticking to the salad. So invest in a salad spinner to dry the greens. If you won't be using the greens right away, dampen them slightly, layer in paper towels, place in a loosely sealed plastic bag to allow for air circulation and store in the crisper drawer of your refrigerator.

When you're ready to assemble your salad, tear leaves into bite-size pieces. If your date has to cut their salad, you haven't done your job. You don't want to get close through the Heimlich maneuver unless, of course, this is one of those games that the two of you like to play. In which case you don't need this book. A therapist, maybe.

Once you've assembled your greens, the fun begins. Go crazy, resist definition, develop your own style. Throw in a few toasted sesame seeds, some pine nuts, pumpkin seeds, a handful of crumbled feta or chèvre (goat cheese).

Try plump, black olives with a few anchovies, sliced fennel with roasted red peppers, or smoked salmon, dill and cucumbers on a bed of bib.

Feeling a little intimidated by the thought of throwing oranges, olives and tuna together? Okay, we'll take it slow. Start with Caesar or Niçoise. The Caesar Salad was invented in the 1920s at Caesar's Hotel in Tiajuanna. Legend has it that the hotel was running out of food, so the chef started grabbing and tossing together ingredients and came up with the first Caesar Salad. This salad could win you an Oscar for presentation if you are willing to assemble the salad live in front of your guest. Niçoise is one of the world's most famous salad combinations: olives, potatoes, green beans, tuna and tomatoes. This salad is so attractive that you may want to arrange the ingredients artistically (called a composed salad) on a large platter instead of tossing them all together.

Now it's time to create your own legacy. Accessorize your salad with chopped herbs, shallots, toasted nuts and seeds. Lemon or lime juice, yogurt, mustard and honey can all be added to dressings to enliven their flavor. Our favorite extras are toasted garlic croutons or toasted pine nuts. Other favorite additions include pasta, shrimp, chopped eggs, capers, roasted red peppers, artichoke hearts, raisins, fennel, new (red) potatoes, chickpeas, grilled chicken, smoked turkey, and marinated or grilled vegetables. Remember, always cut additions into bite-size pieces, and be careful not to overdo it. A perfectly ripe tomato needs only a drop of olive oil and a little salt to bring out its flavor. Let each ingredient speak. You want to create a Mona Lisa not a Liberace.

PLEASE DON'T EAT THE DAISIES

Here are a few of our favorite edible flowers.

Geranium. Geraniums come in many different flavors, including almond, lemon and mint. The flowers smell wonderful, have a mild flavor and are easy to grow.

Nasturtiums. Add the leaves and flowers to salads for a spicy touch.

Roses. They have been consumed for centuries and are believed to bring love. Use the petals in a salad or spike vanilla ice cream with a few drops of rose water (available in Middle Eastern and Indian markets).

Violets. The pink or purple flowers have a somewhat spicy, sweet flavor and are high in vitamins A and C. The leaves and stems are also edible.

Zucchini Blossoms. The bright yellow flowers have a mild flavor and are delicious deep-fried.

Fruit Blossoms (apple, peach, plum), chive blossoms, marigolds and chrysanthemums are other edible floral options.

"What about an Elvis? Iceberg lettuce with fried peanut butter and banana croutons."

"Sorry, Honey. I'd turn in my dietitian's license before I'd make deep fried peanut butter anything"

"Yeah, you're right. What a waste of good peanut butter. Save it for Peanut Butter Biscotti."

CAESAR SALAD

For a main course add a few cooked, sliced sweet Italian sausages or cubes of grilled chicken. For easy last minute prep, tear lettuce leaves and make dressing and croutons ahead of time.

1 medium head romaine lettuce
1 large garlic clove, pressed
3 tablespoons lemon juice
6 anchovy fillets, drained and finely
    chopped
1 teaspoon Dijon mustard
1 teaspoon Worcestershire sauce
⅓ cup olive oil
⅓ cup Parmesan cheese, freshly grated
    (Bottled, preground cheese need
    not apply.)
2 cups Garlic Croutons (recipe follows)
Freshly ground black pepper, to taste

1. Tear the lettuce leaves into bite-size pieces.

2. For the dressing, mix garlic, lemon juice, anchovies, mustard and Worcestershire sauce in a small bowl. Whisk in olive oil with a fork. Dressing can also be mixed in a food processor or blender by processing dressing ingredients until well blended.

3. To assemble bring the torn lettuce leaves, dressing, cheese, croutons and pepper to the table. Pour dressing over greens and toss. Add croutons, sprinkle with cheese and toss. Serve immediately with freshly ground pepper.

GARLIC CROUTONS

Fresh croutons will elevate any salad to a new level. Once you've tasted The Cooking Couple's Garlic Croutons, you'll never go back to store bought. They require four ingredients that you should always have on hand. They can be made a few days ahead and stored in an airtight container or frozen. Impressing your date/mate has never been easier.

1 tablespoon olive oil
1 tablespoon butter
2 garlic cloves, pressed
5 slices day-old Italian or French bread, cut into ½-inch cubes

1. Preheat oven to 300°F.

2. Heat the oil and butter in a medium sauté pan over medium heat. Add the garlic and cook for 1 minute. Add the bread cubes and stir to coat with garlic mixture.

3. Place bread on rimmed cookie sheet, and bake until crisp and golden brown, about 30 minutes.

SALAD NIÇOISE

A loaf of bread, a bottle of white wine and a piece of brie turn this salad into a late-night, romantic supper that will leave you light enough for the fun to come.

¾ pounds new (red) potatoes, about 3
¾ pound green beans, trimmed
¼ cup olive oil
2 tablespoons freshly squeezed lemon juice
¼ teaspoon dried thyme
½ teaspoon champagne mustard
Salt and freshly ground black pepper, to taste
1 small head Bib or Boston lettuce
1 large, ripe tomato, cut into eighths
1 (6⅛ ounce) can tuna, drained and flaked
2 hard boiled eggs, quartered
½ cup pitted black olives, preferably niçoise
2 tablespoons capers, drained
2 tablespoons fresh parsley, minced

1. Scrub the potatoes (no need to peel), and cut into ¼-inch slices. Put the potatoes in a pot, cover with water and add about 1 teaspoon salt. Bring to a boil. Cook until the potatoes are tender, about 20 minutes. Drain the potatoes and run under cold water.

2. Bring 2 quarts water mixed with 1 teaspoon salt to a boil. Prepare an ice bath by filling a large bowl with ice and water. When the water boils drop in the string beans and cook until beans turn bright green, about 1–2 minutes. Drain the beans and place in the ice bath.

3. For the dressing, in a small bowl whisk together the olive oil, lemon juice, thyme and champagne mustard. Add salt and pepper to taste.

4. Wash and dry the lettuce, rip into small pieces and place in a salad bowl or arrange on a plate for a composed salad. Add the potatoes, green beans, tomato, tuna, eggs, olives, capers and parsley. Serve with lemon and olive oil dressing.

FETA AND SEAFOOD PASTA SALAD

Tote this salad to your next picnic.

2 tablespoons olive oil
2 tablespoons lemon juice
1 tablespoon balsamic vinegar
1 teaspoon Dijon mustard
¼ cup parsley, finely chopped
1 tablespoon dried basil
½ teaspoon dried oregano
1 tablespoon fennel seeds
1 cup broccoli florets
3 cups cooked pasta (Shells, rotini and penne work well.)
¼ cup black olives, sliced
½ red pepper, diced
½ cup red onion, chopped
½ cup feta cheese, cubed
8 ounces imitation crab meat, cubed
Salt and freshly ground black pepper, to taste

1. For the dressing, combine the olive oil, lemon juice, vinegar, Dijon mustard, parsley, basil, oregano and fennel seeds in a small bowl or glass jar.
2. In a medium-size bowl, combine the broccoli florets, pasta, black olives, red pepper, red onion, feta cheese and crab meat. Toss with dressing. Add salt and pepper, to taste. Chill and serve.

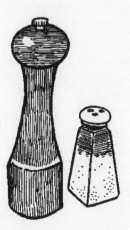

SALAD DRESSINGS You can turn to Kraft or Good Seasons in desperation, but whipping up your own salad dressing takes only a few minutes and greatly improves your salad.

BASIC VINAIGRETTE

⅔ cup olive oil
⅓ cup vinegar
Salt and freshly ground black pepper, to taste

1. Whisk together oil and vinegar. Add salt and pepper, to taste. Mix well before serving.

Variations:

❧ Replace ⅓ cup olive oil with an interesting oil, such as walnut.
❧ Reduce vinegar to 2–3 tablespoons and add 3–4 tablespoons lemon, lime or orange juice.
❧ Add 1 teaspoon chopped shallots or garlic.
❧ Add 2 tablespoons minced herbs.
❧ Add 1 teaspoon Dijon mustard and or 1 tablespoon honey.

Example: Hazelnut Champagne Vinaigrette
>   ⅓ cup olive oil
>   ⅓ cup hazelnut oil
>   ⅓ cup champagne vinegar
>   1 teaspoon chopped shallots

BASIC ORIENTAL DRESSING

Great over greens, bean sprouts, shredded carrots and sliced cucumbers with toasted sesame seeds.

>   2 tablespoons olive oil
>   2 tablespoons toasted sesame oil
>   1 tablespoon soy sauce
>   ¼ cup rice wine vinegar
>   1 teaspoon sugar

1. Whisk together all ingredients.

Variations:

❧ Add ½–1 teaspoon hot chili oil or ¼–½ teaspoon crushed red pepper.
❧ Add 1 teaspoon grated gingerroot.

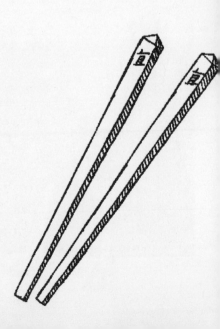

12

Grazing Trays

"Eating with a knife and fork is like making love through a translator."

— Indian saying

"**I**'m not cooking. NO way, NO how, ABSOLUTELY NOT," you say. "But honey I'm hungry, I'm tired, I cooked on Thursday. What's for dinner?" Your partner, who was your lover until the "what's for dinner" conversation started, whines on like a five-year-old. No one wants to cook, and no one is going to buckle down and start up the stove. You have two choices: Argue and starve or give your can opener a workout and concoct a Cooking Couple Grazing Tray.

A grazing tray? Haute cuisine for sheep? We're not talking about frolicking around the dinner table with a bunch of four hoofed, fuzzy friends (unless of course you're into that kind of thing, in which case you bought the wrong book). A grazing tray consists of an endless variety of appetizers, meats, cheeses, dips, spreads and breads designed to tantalize your taste buds throughout the evening. It can be as simple as cheddar and pepperoni on crackers or as elegant as stuffed grape leaves, smoked salmon and canapés. The idea is to lay out an assortment of interesting nibbles and let them fire romance.

Think of the evening as a catered affair for two. Make or buy everything ahead of time so all you'll have to do is lay out the food and party. Concentrate on finger food. Besides cutting down on dirty dishes, eating with your fingers is sexy. Don't take our word for it, just rent *Tom Jones* and bring a napkin.

Take the opportunity to treat yourself to special foods that you don't eat every day. Open a can of smoked oysters. Dig into that jar of Vidalia sweet onion salsa that your mother gave you for Christmas. Try a new cheese with a name you can't pronounce.

Slice a mango or some Jerusalem artichokes. Splurge on a pound of jumbo shrimp. Wrap a round of brie with puff pastry, bake and enjoy the melted treasure that emerges 20 minutes later.

Choose a selection of cold and hot hors d'oeuvres or serve crudités (that's French for cut-up vegetables) and pita bread with Aiolo (garlic mayonnaise), blue cheese dip or hummus. Try tomatoes topped with fresh buffalo mozzarella and basil or a plate of quesadillas. Chicken wings, celery sticks and stuffed potato skins might fit the bill for an autumn romp after the football game. To top off dinner, splurge on several fabulous desserts or a pint of perfectly ripe berries with some sweetened whipped cream.

Generally, we start building our tray with cut-up vegetables. Most supermarkets sell prewashed, peeled and cut-up vegetables and/or have a salad bar so lazy people don't have to scrape and chop. Next, add one or two dips. You can mix your own with a little mayo, sour cream or yogurt or buy a good quality packaged variety.

A CATERED AFFAIR FOR TWO

There's no such thing as a mistake when it comes to putting together a grazing tray. We've paired steamed mussels with ham & cheese croissants and smoked salmon with salsa & chips. If it works do it. Here are some combinations that work for us...

• **Mexican Platter.** For south of the border fish & chips, top blue and yellow corn chips with guacamole and a whole peeled, cooked shrimp. Drizzle with lemon or lime juice. Add salsa, black bean dip and cubes of cheddar.

• **Tall, Dark & Handsome Platter.** A plate of smoked turkey, smoked mozzarella, salami, prosciutto and roast beef served with lettuce, tomato, red onion, Russian dressing, Dijon mustard, dark rye and French bread.

• **Middle Eastern Platter.** This one's easy. Pair hummus, tabbouleh, feta cheese and stuffed grape leaves with toasted pita bread.

• **Smoked Seafood Platter.** Set out a plate of lox with bagels, cream cheese and slices of onion and tomato. Buy a tin of smoked oysters or mussels and serve with crackers and smoked bluefish or mackerel. Accompany with mustard/dill mayo. (Mix 1/4 cup mayo with 1 table-spoon lemon juice, 1 tablespoon mustard and 1 teaspoon fresh, chopped dill.)

• **Antipasto Platter.** Cooked cheese tortellini on skewers with tomato sauce for dipping, roasted red peppers and artichokes surrounded by black olives, cured meats, fresh mozzarella, marinated or stuffed mushrooms, Eggplant Sandwiches and Italian peppers.

• **Lite-Bite Platter.** Prosciutto wrapped around sliced melon, crudités with Aiola, cheese and crackers and peel & eat shrimp with cocktail sauce.

Pretend you're on a treasure hunt searching for the most delicious food you can find. The best discoveries often lurk in the frozen food section: tiny egg rolls, gourmet pizza, stuffed clams, pierogies and quiche. If you've got a hankering for shrimp or smoked turkey, move over to the deli. You may also find some tasty prepared salads or goodies for dessert. Check out ethnic foods. Your store may carry Middle Eastern (baba ganjoush, spinach turnovers, hummus, stuffed grape leaves), Jewish (knishes, herring, lox, bagels) or Mexican (chips, salsa, black bean dip, burritos) delicacies. Look for caponata (eggplant dip) available in the canned vegetable section of many grocery stores to spread on crackers or use as a dip. Visit the cheese section and don't forget French bread.

In the mood for just a little cooking? Defrost a package of puffed pastry Set the oven to 375°F. Roll the pastry into a 12 x 8-inch rectangle. Sprinkle half the dough with grated cheese. Fold the dough over, brush with a little beaten egg, bake until golden brown (about 15 minutes) and cut into squares. Try our quick, unusual recipe for Falafel Wings, or turn a loaf of French bread into Broccoli Crostini.

Don't feel like fixing dinner? Cooking should never be a chore, so both of you get the night off. No boning and pounding chicken breasts, no stirring sauces, no grouchy faces. Just a rendezvous for two satisfied stomachs and twenty sticky fingers.

HERB STUFFED MUSHROOMS

These are so good that Michael, who's allergic to mushrooms, is tempted to take a bite. These can be prepared and refrigerated ahead of time and broiled at the last minute. You can make our recipe for Herb Cheese or buy boursin or another prepared herb cheese.

16 large mushrooms
1 cup (16 ounces) Herb Cheese (see page 26.)

1. Wash the mushrooms well. Remove the stems, being careful not to break the caps. Preheat broiler.

2. Place about 1 tablespoon cheese in each mushroom cap. Place mushrooms on lightly greased broiler pan.

3. Broil 4–5 inches from the heat until golden brown, about 4–5 minutes.

Variation: Italian Style Stuffed Mushrooms. Follow the recipe above. Instead of Herb Cheese, stuff the mushrooms with the following mixture: 1 cup Italian bread crumbs, 1 pressed garlic clove, ¼ cup milk, ¼ cup pine nuts, 1 teaspoon dried basil and 2 tablespoons fresh minced parsley. Sprinkle with Parmesan cheese before broiling.

BROCCOLI CROSTINI

This Mediterranean inspired starter is perfect for hot summer nights.

1 (12-inch) loaf Italian bread, cut into 24 slices
3 garlic cloves
1 tablespoon olive oil
1 medium onion, chopped
2½ cups broccoli florets, chopped
2 tablespoons tomato paste
1 medium tomato, chopped
¼ cup sun-dried tomatoes, reconstituted in boiling water and chopped
¼ cup olives, chopped
2 teaspoons anchovy paste (Don't worry if you hate anchovies — this
    just adds flavor.)
1 tablespoon balsamic vinegar
¼ cup fresh parsley, chopped
1 teaspoon dried oregano
Salt and freshly ground black pepper, to taste

1. Rub the Italian bread slices with a halved garlic clove. Toast the bread in a 350°F oven until golden brown, about 10 minutes.

2. Heat the olive oil in a large sauté pan over medium heat. Add the onion and sauté until soft, about 5–6 minutes.

3. Chop the 2 remaining garlic cloves and add to the pan along with broccoli. Reduce heat to medium-low. Cook, stirring occasionally, until broccoli starts to soften, about 5 minutes. Add tomato (paste, fresh and sun-dried), olives, anchovy paste, vinegar, parsley, oregano, salt and pepper. Cook, stirring occasionally, until all vegetables are soft, about 5 minutes.

4. To serve, spread the bread slices with the vegetable mixture. Top with grated Romano or Parmesan cheese, if desired.

QUESADILLAS

These are great grilled. Create a few different varieties and serve with crudités for a great Grazing Tray.

> 6 flour tortillas
> 4 ounces Monterey jack or pepper jack cheese, grated (about 1 cup)
> 1 bunch scallions, chopped (optional)
> Salsa
> Guacamole (recipe follows)

1. Preheat a grill or lightly-greased skillet over medium heat.
2. Lay out 1 tortilla. Cover half the tortilla with about 2½ tablespoons cheese. Sprinkle the same half with chopped scallions. Fold tortilla over. Repeat for remaining tortillas.
3. Place the quesadillas directly on preheated grill or skillet. Cook first side until golden brown, about 2 minutes. Flip over and cook until cheese is melted and both sides are golden brown.
4. Cut in wedges and serve with salsa and Guacamole.

Variations:

- **Ham & Cheese Quesadillas.** Add ½ cup chopped, boiled Danish ham to the recipe.
- **Haute Cuisine Quesadillas.** Use 1 cup crumbled chèvre (goat cheese), instead of the Monterey or pepper jack, with 2 tablespoons chopped roasted red peppers, 3 tablespoons minced cilantro and 1 teaspoon minced jalapeno pepper.
- **Tomato Chicken.** Add 1 diced grilled chicken breast and ½ cup chopped tomatoes to the recipe.
- **Veggie.** Sauté ½ medium onion, ½ cup sliced mushrooms and ½ cup chopped peppers and add to the recipe.

GUACAMOLE

Great on chips, nachos, burgers, crudités and quesadillas.

> 1 ripe avocado
> 1 teaspoon lemon or lime juice
> 1 small garlic clove, pressed or finally minced
> 1 tablespoon onion, grated
> ½ jalapeno pepper, chopped or a pinch cayenne pepper (optional)

1. Cut avocado in half. Remove pit and scoop out flesh. Mash with remaining ingredients until smooth.

FALAFEL WINGS

Chicken can marinate in yogurt for several hours to tenderize the wings.

> 8–12 chicken wings
> 1 cup yogurt
> 1 cup falafel mix
> ½ cup sesame seeds

1. Mix chicken with yogurt.
2. Mix falafel mix with sesame seeds.
3. Preheat oven to 400°F.
4. Dip wings into falafel and sesame seed mixture. Place wings on foil-lined baking pan, and bake until tender and cooked through, about 35–40 minutes.

SPINACH PILLOWS

This classic, classy finger food comes straight to you from the Mediterranean. Make extra and freeze for quick, effortless entertaining.

1 tablespoon vegetable oil
1 medium onion, chopped
10 ounces frozen, chopped spinach, defrosted
1 cup ricotta cheese
1 cup feta cheese, crumbled
1 tablespoon flour
1 egg, lightly beaten
½ teaspoon dried basil
¼ teaspoon dried oregano
Salt and freshly ground black pepper, to taste
½ package phyllo dough (12 sheets)
¼ cup olive oil

1. Heat 1 tablespoon vegetable oil in a sauté pan over medium heat. Add the onion and sauté until soft, about 5 minutes.

2. Drain the spinach and squeeze out as much liquid as possible. Combine the sautéed onion, spinach, ricotta cheese, feta cheese, flour, egg, basil, oregano, salt and pepper.

3. Preheat the oven to 350°F. Grease a baking sheet.

4. Uncover the phyllo dough. (Make sure to keep dough covered with a damp cloth while you work so it doesn't dry out.) Lay one sheet phyllo dough on a large cutting board and using a pastry brush, paint on a thin layer of olive oil. Cover with another sheet of dough and another layer of olive oil. Repeat for a third sheet of dough.

5. Cut the dough into 3 strips lengthwise with a sharp knife. Place 2 tablespoons filling at the end of each strip. Fold a corner across dough and continue folding, as if you were folding a flag, until you have formed a triangle. Place on prepared baking sheet. Repeat with remaining dough.

6. Brush with additional olive oil, and bake until golden brown, about 25 minutes.

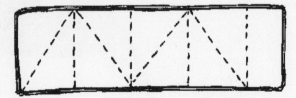

13

Dracula's Last Kiss

"I felt myself rising, as if I were floating in the darkness, and then the darkness, like the heartbeat, began to fade."

—*Louis from* Interview with the Vampire
by Anne Rice

*F*angs press into soft, pliant flesh. A murmur, a sigh, a moan. Vampires, creatures of the night, are sensual, mysterious and pushy. You don't want Dracula dropping in when you're weaving your own erotic spell. You may be cute, but the Count doesn't take no for an answer.

To repel these tuxedoed party crashers, we recommend *Alum sativum,* or to you folks who didn't get an A in botany, garlic. Its power to deter evil is legendary and its impact on mortals is, shall we say noticeable?

The Egyptians fed their slaves garlic to give them strength and recorded 22 garlic remedies as early as 1500 B.C. to cure ailments from headaches to heart problems. Roman soldiers ate garlic for courage, and Hippocrates prescribed garlic for illnesses. Louis Pasteur investigated garlic's natural antibiotic properties, and for centuries garlic was used to treat wounded soldiers. Scientific studies suggest that garlic may boost the immune system and memory, decrease heart disease and cancer risk and battle viruses and bacteria. Think of that the next time you complain your mate has garlic breath.

Garlic has influenced world cuisine for centuries. Romans, the Johnny Apple Seeds of garlic, spread heads of garlic in their wake (as well as anyone else's head that got in the way) as they conquered the ancient world. Garlic is still an international giant used in most cuisines. In China, garlic is stir-fried with a variety of meats and vegetables to create hot and spicy dishes like garlic shrimp, stir-fried beef with garlic and garlic-flavored long beans. The first step in most Italian dishes is: Sauté garlic in olive oil. In France, Aioli (garlic mayonnaise) accompanies fish, vegetables and bread. The Cooking Couple

ROASTED GARLIC

Roasted garlic makes a wonderful creamy dip or addition to foods from cheese spreads to mashed potatoes. Try it on bread, with goats' cheese on crackers or mix with hummus or cream cheese.

  3–4 garlic bulbs
  1 tablespoon olive oil

1. Peel away the outside layer of the garlic bulbs, leaving the skin surrounding the cloves and the head itself intact. Cut off about 1/4-inch from the top of each bulb and brush with olive oil.

2. Wrap garlic bulbs in aluminum foil, place in a 350°F oven or toaster oven and bake until soft, about 45 minutes to an hour. Let cool. To serve, squeeze the soft garlic out of the top of the cloves. You can mix the roasted garlic pulp with additional olive oil (1–2 tablespoons), oregano (about 1/2 teaspoon dried) and a little water (1–2 tablespoons) for a sauce, dressing or spread.

VAMPIRES CRAVE VARIETY

Even vampires get sick of the same old thing for dinner every night. We have it on good authority that when Lestat wants something different to drink he reaches for After Shock, Hot & Cool Cinnamon Liquor. It's served chilled, tastes like a cinnamon red hot going down and packs a mean buzz. The liquor starts out at 80 proof and as edible crystals grow in the bottle it can get as high as 90. You can try it for yourself, talk to Lestat or chat with After Shock on the Internet at HTTP://WWW.VIBE.C.

couldn't live without garlic. We use it in many of our recipes and go through 4–5 bulbs a month, especially during cold season when a clove a day seems to help keep colds and flu away.

The flavor and smell of garlic make it a valuable seasoning. But if your dining partner isn't a fan of the odoriferous bulb, you may not get past the dishes. Caution should be exercised when using all seasonings, especially garlic. Too much can be the kiss of death. But what a lovely demise.

Garlic's aroma is released when the cloves are peeled and minced. (For easy preparation squash a clove with the back of a wide knife and remove the skin.) Raw garlic is extremely strong. Fortunately, cooking sweetens garlic's pungent punch without effecting its medicinal value. Don't eat or serve it raw unless you and your date are garlic freaks like us. Check out your partner's garlic tolerance early in the relationship. Some people eat garlic in everything including ice cream. We've even seen recipes for chocolate dipped garlic cloves. Others prefer garlic in soup, scampi or any number of meat and fish dishes. That's the beauty of this magical orb. Garlic brings its mystical power to any dish it kisses.

Craftily conceal your garlic and chances are your dining companion will not notice its presence. If your date becomes outraged because you threw in a clove or two, examine your companion's canines and sleeping habits. Remember, garlic is meant to be shared. Garlic breath is only fun when both parties partake.

To awaken the senses and send Dracula back to the grave, use fresh garlic which is available year round. Instant, granulated and garlic salt are poor imitations and can have rancid overtones. Look for plump, firm bulbs and store them in a cool, dry, dark place.

If your partner's not a garlic lover, rub your hands in coffee grounds or around the rim of a damp stainless-steel sink to get rid of the smell. To keep your lover from fleeing, freshen your breath by munching on parsley or a whole coffee bean.

GREMOLATA

Gremolata is a sassy Italian sauce made from garlic, parsley and lemon. Try gremolata tossed with steamed or boiled vegetables or serve with chilled, cooked shellfish.

To make about 1/4 cup gremolata combine 2 finely minced cloves garlic, 2 tablespoons finely minced fresh Italian parsley and 1 tablespoon finely grated lemon peel.

You don't need recipes to start incorporating garlic into dishes. Throw some on a roast, in a soup, salad dressing or stew, or season your salad bowl by rubbing a clove into the wood. Sauté garlic in a little olive oil and add to broccoli, potatoes or bread. (Garlic and olive oil go together like coffee and chocolate or lemon and fish.) Bake or roast a head of garlic right in its skin and squeeze the soft pulp into sauces, soups or mashed potatoes, or use as a dip or spread.

The following recipes are guaranteed to keep even Lestat at bay. But then again, he's such a charming fellow.

SPANISH GARLIC SOUP

The beautiful aroma that waifs through the kitchen is reason enough to create this potent brew. This soup is addictive. Once you reach the treasures at the bottom of your bowl, you'll know why.

    1 tablespoon olive oil
    6 large garlic cloves, minced
    ½ teaspoon paprika
    4 cups chicken broth
    ½ teaspoon oregano
    1 tablespoon fresh parsley, finely minced
    Salt and freshly ground black pepper, to taste
    4 slices French or Italian bread
    2 eggs
    2 tablespoons Parmesan or Romano cheese, grated

1. Heat the oil over low heat in a pot large enough to hold 4 cups broth. Add the garlic and sauté, stirring gently, until the garlic starts to turn golden brown, about 5 minutes.

2. Add the paprika, continue to stir and cook for another 1–2 minutes. Add the chicken broth and oregano, and bring to a simmer. Simmer covered for about 15 minutes.

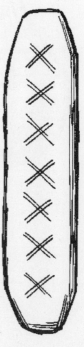

3. While the soup cooks, toast the bread in a 350°F oven until golden brown.

4. Preheat the oven to 425°F. Add the parsley and salt and pepper to taste to the soup.

5. Place bread in two oven-proof soup bowls. (We use classic French onion soup bowls.) Ladle in the soup, making sure to divide the broth and garlic evenly between the bowls. Carefully crack an egg into each bowl. (The egg will slip to the bottom.) Sprinkle each bowl with 1 tablespoon cheese. Place in the oven and bake for 2–3 minutes.

GOLDEN GARLIC VEGETABLES

Sautéing garlic to a golden brown brings out the bulb's warm, earthy nature. Golden garlic provides the perfect blanket of flavor for many cooked vegetables.

> 1 tablespoon olive oil
> 6 large garlic cloves, sliced

> 1. Heat the oil over medium heat in a sauté pan.
> 2. Add the garlic and sauté until garlic is golden brown (about 3 minutes), being careful not to let garlic burn.
> 3. Toss with your favorite cooked vegetables.

How to cook vegetables such as broccoli, asparagus, carrots, snow peas or string beans...

- **Steamed.** Cut vegetables into bite-size pieces. Set vegetables in a steamer basket or rack. Place the rack in a wok or pot. Pour boiling water into the pan about 1-inch from the bottom of the steamer. Cover and bring the water back to a boil. Cook for a few minutes until vegetables are bright green and crisp. Toss with golden garlic, salt and pepper.

- **Stir-fried.** Cut vegetables into bite-size pieces. Heat 1 tablespoon vegetable oil (peanut oil works well) in a wok or sauté pan over high heat. Add the vegetables, turn heat down to medium high and cook until vegetables turn bright green. (If you want a hot dish, add ¼ teaspoon crushed red pepper with the vegetables.) Toss with golden garlic. We also like this dish mixed with 1 tablespoon oyster or soy sauce and 1 teaspoon toasted sesame oil.

How to cook cherry tomatoes...
Heat 1 tablespoon olive oil in a sauté pan over medium heat. Add a pint stemmed cherry tomatoes. Sauté for 2–3 minutes until tomatoes are soft but not broken. Toss with golden garlic, salt and pepper. You can also add 2–3 tablespoons minced fresh herbs.

AIOLA (GARLIC MAYONNAISE)

Garlic sauces are popular throughout the Mediterranean. Aiola comes from the southeastern region of France called Provence. In summer, entire villages hold food festivals featuring the sauce called the Butter of Provence. Try it with grilled fish, spread it on crusty bread or serve it with steamed or raw vegetables.

> 4–6 garlic cloves*
> 1 cup mayonnaise
> 1 teaspoon lemon juice

1. Peel the garlic. With a mortar and pestle pound the garlic into a smooth paste or process through a garlic press.
2. Stir together garlic, mayonnaise and lemon juice.

* *The amount depends on the size of the cloves, the season of the year and your senses of smell and taste. Garlic is generally more pungent in the spring right after it's harvested. By winter the bulb mellows considerably.*

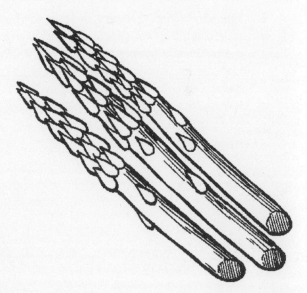

PASTA WITH GARLIC

This works as a main dish when served with a substantial salad or as a side dish with chicken or fish.

½ pound pasta (Spaghetti, fussili, angel hair and linguine work well.)
¼ cup olive oil
4 garlic cloves, minced
¼ cup Parmesan or Romano cheese, grated
Salt and freshly ground black pepper, to taste
2 tablespoons parsley, chopped

1. Boil a pot of salted water, add the pasta and cook until pasta is al dente.
2. Heat the olive oil in a medium sauté pan over low heat. Add the garlic and sauté for 3 minutes. Set sauté pan aside until pasta is done.
3. When the pasta is cooked, drain pasta leaving a little cooking water clinging to the pasta. Transfer the pasta to medium-size serving bowl. Toss with garlic olive oil mixture and grated cheese. Add salt, pepper and parsley.

Variations:

- **Broccoli Garlic Ziti.** Toss in two cups steamed broccoli florets with the pasta, garlic, olive oil and cheese.

- **Angel Hair Pasta with Shrimp and Garlic.** Add ½ pound uncooked medium peeled and deveined shrimp 1 minute after adding the garlic. Cook shrimp until they turn pink, about 3 minutes. Toss with pasta, cheese and 1 tablespoon minced parsley.

- **Spicy Garlic Shrimp with Angel Hair Pasta.** Follow the above recipe and add ¼–½ teaspoon crushed red pepper when you sauté the garlic.

SPICY ORANGE GARLIC BEEF

Better than take-out. Serve with boiled white rice and a bottle of merlot.

¼ cup soy sauce

1 cup orange juice

6 garlic cloves, pressed

½ teaspoon grated gingerroot

¼–½ teaspoon crushed red pepper, depending on how spicy you want the dish

12 ounces sirloin, cut into thin strips for stir-frying

2 tablespoons vegetable oil

2 large onions, cut in half and sliced

1 red pepper, cut into 1-inch pieces

2 cups broccoli florets, cut into bite-size pieces

2 tablespoons cornstarch, mixed with 2 tablespoons water

1 bunch scallions, chopped

1. Mix together the soy sauce, orange juice, garlic, gingerroot and crushed red pepper. Pour over the beef and allow to marinate for several hours or overnight.

2. Heat 1 tablespoon oil in a wok or large sauté pan over medium-high heat. Add the onions and cook until they start to soften, about 5 minutes. Add the fresh red pepper and broccoli. Cook for another few minutes until broccoli turns bright green. Set aside in a covered bowl to keep mixture warm while you cook the beef.

3. Heat remaining tablespoon oil in the wok or sauté pan over high heat. Remove beef from marinade, reserving marinade for final step, and stir-fry until beef is barely cooked through.

4. Add reserved marinade to pan. Bring to a boil, lower heat to a simmer and add cooked vegetables. Cook for another minute to reheat vegetables. Add cornstarch and water mixture and stir well to combine. Continue to stir until the sauce thickens slightly, another 2–3 minutes. Garnish with the chopped scallions and serve over white rice.

14

Caveman's Delight

"I am Tarzan of the Apes. I want you. I am
yours. You are mine."

— *Tarzan, from* Tarzan of the Apes
by Edgar Rice Burroughs

*M*EAT. Grilled racks of ribs, juicy flame-broiled burgers, 24-ounce porterhouse steaks. The craving rises with the full moon and the first warm days of spring. The smell of barbecue wafts over the neighborhood. The skin on the back of your neck tightens, the hairs bristle, a primal instinct from deep within your subconscious gnaws at your soul. You've got to have meat now.

You peer over the fence and watch as your neighbor smothers the crimson slab in rich, thick sauce. He goes inside. Now, do it now. Like a cougar with the scent for supper, you bolt the fence, grab the steak and run howling to your lair.

There's no stopping the Caveman. Luckily you're a fully grown homo-sapien so you can appease that appetite before the neighbors have you arrested for howling at the moon and stealing steaks. No need to throw rocks or spears to nab dinner. Get to the store or preferably the butcher, and purchase the thickest, biggest, juiciest steak you can find 'cause summer's here and the time is right for barbecue, the great American pastime. Build that fire, toss on the raw beef and salivate as the steaks cook slowly over smoky coals.

Forget vegetables (except for our wonderful Grilled Vegetable recipe). This is no time for carrots and cauliflower. It is time for tender, juicy, succulent meat, preferably on the bone, smothered in tangy, spicy sauce. A grilled ear of corn slathered with butter and a side of spicy beans are all you'll want. If you're a meat and potatoes lover, try The Cooking Couple's Garlic Grilled Taters with a side of charred zucchini.

No sex until you've gorged yourself; you're too hungry. Tending and devouring that succulent, sweet flesh requires your full attention. Once you're fed and have an hour to digest your food, you'll pick up a different scent.

Meat works wonders on your libido and your brain. After a high protein meal, your blood stream is flooded with the amino acid tyrosine. The chemicals made from tyrosine, dopamine and norepinephrine, trigger brain cells that enhance mental alertness and concentration.

"Ellen, stop reading your physiology book and pass the steak sauce."

Some scientists believe that the move from a vegetarian diet to a plant and meat-based diet (which occurred when early man started hunting approximately 2.5 million years ago) sparked cerebral growth. According to a report in *Current Anthropology,* before our ancestors began eating protein and calorie-rich meat, huge amounts of energy were needed by the stomach and intestines to extract nutrients from plant foods. With the introduction of protein-rich, easy-to-digest meat, the digestive system shrunk and extra energy was available to power brain growth.

GET THEM RIBS

Tired of mosquitoes, smoke in your eyes and getting burned by hot grease? Then turn off the grill and pick up the phone for the best baby back ribs in the world. We discovered 'em at Carson's in Chicago. Not in the Windy City? Neither are we.

Lucky for us, and you, they deliver anywhere, over-night via Federal Express. Just call 1-800-GET-RIBS.

So if you can plan your party a day in advance, have the best there is and let someone else get bit by the skeeters.

"So how come lions don't play chess and write sensitive poetry?"
"Because they're just like men."
"But I write sensitive poetry and play chess."
"You're the exception to the rule. That's why I married you."
"I thought we married each other."
"Silly boy. Pass the toothpicks please."

With your brain and body fueled and your libido howling, it's time for dessert. After gorging yourself on meat, you're going to want something a little more substantial than watermelon. So, grab your partner, do-si-do upstairs to that little old corral, strap on your spurs and ride 'em cowgirl. Yee ha!

GRILLED STEAK

The best way to cook a great, tender, well-marbled steak is to brush the meat with olive oil, rub it with a little salt and freshly ground black pepper, sear it quickly on a well-oiled, hot grill (to seal in the juices), cook on one side, flip and cook until it's done to your liking.

The easiest way to tell when meat is done is to use a thermometer. (Caution, piercing a steak with anything allows some juices to escape.) As you become more experienced, you may be able to tell when a steak is done by touching the meat. Rare meat feels like the top of the fleshy area between your thumb and index finger when your hand is relaxed. Medium feels like the same area when you make a fist. Clench your fist tightly and you'll have an idea how well-done meat feels to the touch. A 1¹/₂-inch steak done medium takes about six minutes per a side.

The best quality (juiciest, most flavorful and tender) grade of meat with the most marbling (the thin veins of fat that run through a piece of meat) is prime. Prime is usually expensive, well-aged and sold in restaurants not grocery stores. Choice is easier to find and usually has enough marbling to produce a flavorful, tender steak. Look for New York, T-bone, filet mignon and porterhouse steaks that are 1¹/₄ to 3-inches thick.

Leaner cuts (London broil, flank and round steak) are also great on the grill, but they should be marinated for several hours to increase flavor and tenderness. They generally take longer to cook than well-marbled, aged steaks.

Hamburgers are always a great grilling option. To make burgers special, mix chopped herbs or onion into the meat before grilling. Top with sliced tomato, pickles, herb butter, mustard, ketchup, relish, red onion, lettuce or bacon. When cooking your burgers don't mash them down. Mashing does not make them cook faster. It forces out all the juices so you're left with a dry, leathery slab of meat better suited to a Burger Town drive-through than your barbecue.

GRILLED CHICKEN

Marinate the chicken for 24 hours to infuse the dish with flavor. This marinade also works well with fish and tofu and is fabulous with Rock Cornish game hens. Extra marinade can be boiled for 5 minutes and used to baste chicken as it cooks.

¼ cup orange juice
½ cup soy sauce
2 tablespoons white wine or rice vinegar
1 tablespoon vegetable oil
1 tablespoon honey
1 garlic clove, minced
1 teaspoon grated or ¼ teaspoon powdered gingerroot
1 cut-up whole chicken or assorted pieces

1. Combine the orange juice, soy sauce, vinegar, honey, oil, garlic and gingerroot. Pour over the chicken. Allow to marinate in the refrigerator for at least 4 hours, turning pieces every few hours.

2. When ready to cook preheat grill. Cook chicken for 35–40 minutes turning frequently and basting with boiled marinade. Cooking time depends on the type of grill and what chicken pieces are used.

Variations: Grilled Tofu. To remove some of the moisture from tofu, place 16 ounces firm or extra firm tofu between two plates weighted down with cans or an iron skillet, and let sit for 30 minutes to 1 hour. Cut tofu into 1-inch slices or cubes (for skewers) and place in marinade. Let marinate for 1–2 hours in the refrigerator, turning occasionally. Cook over low heat, basting with additional marinade, until tofu is heated through and golden brown, about 5 minutes per side.

GRILLED SWORDFISH WITH MANGO KIWI SALSA

Swordfish is our favorite fish to grill. This salsa complements the firm-fleshed fish beautifully. This dish works well with Quesadillas and Grilled Vegetables.

1 mango,* peeled and cut into ¼-inch dice
1 kiwi, peeled and cut into ¼-inch dice
1 cup fresh or canned (unsweetened) pineapple, cut into ¼-inch dice
¼ cup red onion, chopped
Pinch of cayenne pepper
1 tablespoon lime juice
2 tablespoons fresh cilantro, minced
Salt and freshly ground black pepper, to taste
2 swordfish steaks (about ½ pound each)
2 teaspoons olive oil

1. In a small bowl, stir together the mango, kiwi, pineapple, red onion, cayenne pepper, lime juice and cilantro. Add salt and pepper to taste.

2. Preheat the grill. Rub the fish with olive oil and sprinkle with salt and pepper. Grill for 4–5 minutes, turn fish and grill for another 4–5 minutes for a total of 8–10 minutes per inch. To test doneness insert a small knife in the thickest part of the fish and make sure flesh is opaque all the way through. Serve with salsa.

*Mangos are available from May to September. (Peak month is June.) The sweetest mangos have skins tinged with orange and red. Avoid green mangos, they may not ripen properly; and mangos with brown spots, they're too ripe. Mangos are ripe when they smell fragrant and are slightly soft. Underripe mangos should be kept at room temperature until slightly soft and fragrant. Ripe mangos belong in the refrigerator. To speed the ripening process, place mango in a paper bag that has a few holes in it.

To prepare your mango cut vertically all the way around. Peel off the skin and cut the flesh into strips. Remember, mangos are messy so enjoy the fruit with a friend.

GRILLED VEGETABLES

Most vegetables, from artichokes to zucchini, are great on the grill. Some of our favorites include broccoli, cherry tomatoes, summer squash, snow peas, onions, mushrooms, peppers, garlic cloves, carrots and asparagus. Use our marinade or simply pour about ½ cup of your favorite salad dressing (not the creamy type) over the veggies or brush lightly with olive oil right before grilling, squeeze with lemon juice as they cook and serve with Aioli (garlic mayonnaise).

   About 3–4 cups assorted vegetables
   1 teaspoon prepared mustard
   2 garlic cloves, crushed
   ½ cup vinegar, lemon or lime juice
   ¼ cup olive oil
   2 tablespoons chopped fresh herbs or 1 teaspoon dried herbs
   ¼ teaspoon salt
   ¼ teaspoon freshly ground black pepper

   1. Cut the vegetables into bite-size pieces.*
   2. Combine mustard, garlic, vinegar (or lemon or lime juice), olive oil, salt and pepper. Pour over vegetables and let marinate for no more than ½ hour.
   3. Grill vegetables over a medium-hot fire, turning frequently, until vegetables are tender and brown on the outside and sweet inside, about 10–20 minutes.

Large vegetables (greater than ½-inch thick, such as onions, summer squash and peppers) can be sliced or quartered. Cut delicate vegetables (fennel, asparagus, summer squash, mushrooms, tomatoes) into larger pieces than dense vegetables (turnips, onions, carrots, broccoli and peppers). Large vegetables (zucchini, onions and eggplant) can also be cut in half and placed directly on the grill. You can purchase a grilling basket that goes directly on top of the grill and keeps vegetables from slipping into the fire. Delicate vegetables should be added to the basket later in the cooking process to keep them from getting overdone. Vegetables can also be cooked on skewers.

GARLIC GRILLED TATERS

Whatever we're grilling, we almost never go without a batch of these delicious spuds.

 1 tablespoons olive oil
 1 teaspoon dried oregano
 6 garlic cloves, pressed
 ½ teaspoon Kosher or sea salt
 ¼ teaspoon freshly ground black pepper
 4 baking potatoes

1. Preheat grill. Mix together the oil, oregano, garlic, salt and pepper.

2. Scrub, wash and dry the potatoes and cut in half the long way. Rub the potatoes all over with the oil mixture. Reserve any remaining mixture.

3. Grill the potatoes, turning and basting with extra oil mixture, until potatoes are brown and soft when pierced with a fork, about 20 minutes.

15

Where's the Beef?

"If cannibals ate a lot of turnips it wouldn't make them vegetarians."

— *William, from the film* Paris, France

You're a meat-loving American. For years it's been meatloaf, meatballs, meat pies, meat and potatoes, corned beef, cheeseburgers, chuck and sirloin. Now your passion for red, rare beef has been usurped by a fire-breathing, tattooed goddess with a bad attitude and more nose rings than Ferdinand the Bull. She looks like she could devour you and a T-bone steak simultaneously. But, she's a vegetarian. Meat is murder. She'll party till dawn, but don't even think about getting her to share your pepperoni pizza or try your mother's meatloaf. A relationship with her means brussel sprouts, brown rice, the stereo on 11, slam dancing, midnight horror movies, bad punk bands and black beans till death or indigestion, do you part.

This could be a good thing. Have you looked into your arteries lately? Do they resemble the Lincoln Tunnel during New York City rush hour? If so, you could use a heaping plate of beans and greens.

We understand you have misgivings about going meatless. Michael and I were together for almost a year before I unleashed the veggie fare. These are not dinners to try early on in the relationship unless you know your date's a vegetarian or attended the original Woodstock. The first time I served Michael my vegetarian melange, I thought it was all over. "This isn't funny. If I wanted to eat like this, I would have joined the Hare Krishnas," he said after surveying his plate.

After two bites, much to my surprise and delight, he stopped sneering, started making slurping noises and asked for seconds. We dined on roasted onions, spicy squash and lentil stew by candlelight and went to bed full but not stuffed.

HIGH CHOLESTEROL AND ERECTILE DYSFUNCTION

According to a study in the *American Journal of Epidemiology,* men with high cholesterol levels (over 240) have 1.83 times the risk of erectile dysfunction as men with lower cholesterol levels.

Now we have your attention. While occasionally indulging in the previous chapter's delights is fine, the era of eating 24-ounce porterhouse steaks, four days a week with a baked potato swimming in an artery-choking pool of butter are over.

Most saturated fats, the type of fat that raises blood cholesterol, are found in full-fat dairy products (like butter and ice cream) and fatty meats (like prime rib, leg of lamb and chicken skin). So, to stay trim and keep your arteries from resembling rusty, clogged pipes, limit your intake of fat, saturated fat and cholesterol. Try eating vegetarian meals several times a week. Eat less meat and enjoy it more when you do.

AN APPLE A DAY

By now the link between diet and chronic disease is well established. Here are some suggestions to keep you and your honey bunch healthy.

Fruits & Vegetables. Eat at least five servings a day. They contain antioxidants, which help prevent both cancer and heart disease, and fiber, which can help lower cholesterol levels, prevent certain cancers and keep blood sugar levels even.

Beans & Grains. Eat more beans and grains. Like fruits and most vegetables, they are low-in-fat, high-in-fiber and cholesterol-free. Fruits, vegetables, beans and grains also contain phytochemicals: substances found in plants, with strange names such as genestein (in soy foods like tofu) limonene (in citrus fruits), allyl sulfide (in garlic and onions) and dithiolthione (in broccoli) that may help prevent cancer.

Calcium. Found in dairy products, calcium-fortified foods, green leafy vegetables, tofu and fish eaten with the bones (sardines and canned salmon). Calcium is key in helping prevent the bone disease, osteoporosis. Aim for 1,000 mg a day.

Vegetables are bright, vibrant and sexy. They turn you on without filling you out. Besides being healthy and inexpensive, many vegetarian dishes fit The Cooking Couple's threefold criteria: quick, easy and fun. Plus, vegetarian dishes can be kept on hold for hours. Lasagna doesn't go anywhere until you eat it, and hummus never walks away unless you roll it up in a pita to go. Vegetarian food lends itself to spontaneity. Nuke a baked potato and cover it with a blanket of sassy sauce. Boil pasta and serve with sautéed vegetables. Cook up lentils with an onion, add a few spices, and presto, you have soup. With the exception of fresh produce, most vegetarian ingredients keep for a few weeks to several months.

There really is such a thing as a (cholesterol) free ride when it comes to fruits, vegetables and grains. Vegetarian foods are cholesterol-free and generally low in fat and saturated fat. Just don't fry 'em or drown 'em in cream sauce, margarine, butter or oil. They are high in fiber, that proven cholesterol fighter, and cancer-preventing antioxidents.

Okay, so we have a few rich dishes in this book. Remember, we follow the 20/80 rule: Eat right 80 percent of the time and you get to cheat a little. We don't eat the rich recipes in this book every night (especially fondue, baked brie and brownies). Who has the time or the waistline for it? Often, we dine on vegetable soup or low-fat stir-fries so we can afford the splurges. Vegetarian fare helps make up for the indulgences like the ones in "Caveman's Delight."

WHAT'S A VEGAN?

Not all vegetarians are created equal. Here are the differences to help you decide what to make for dinner if your date says, "I'm a vegetarian."

Vegan. They eat no food of animal origin. You'd better pull out the tofu and tell them to take vitamin B12 supplements. (Except for tiny amounts found on the roots of legumes, B12 is only found in animal foods.)

Ovolactovegetarian. They will eat milk and eggs, so quiche is just fine. Just leave out the bacon.

Pescovegetarian. They eat fish, but no other food of animal origin. Try our recipe for Grilled Swordfish.

Ovo-lacto-pollovegetarian. They eat chicken, eggs and milk. Say it three times fast and you may choke.

Fruitarians. They avoid all foods of animal origin along with vegetables and grains (i.e., all they eat is fruit, honey and nuts). Good luck fixing dinner.

She's 5'3", weighs 100 pounds, is cute as a button and runs a 5:40 mile. She's what you've always been looking for. You invite her over for dinner. She says, "Yes, great. Oh, by the way, I don't eat meat." "No problem, neither do I," you lie. All you know how to do is broil a chop, grill sirloin and flip burgers. You've got to impress her, but she say's she's a total vegan. You remind yourself to watch *Star Trek* so you'll know what that is, but first you gotta come up with something for dinner.

These recipes will impress both of you and they're easy. If you're scared about cutting your teeth on Spiced Teff with Arame or Quinoa Vegetable Paella, start with familiar dishes like chili or pasta. If you're looking to convert your date, these recipes are a great place to start. They're so good that neither of you will ask "Where's the beef?"

HOOKER PASTA

This recipe, known as Pasta Puttanesca, was named for the puttane (Italian prostitutes) who often ate a version of the dish when they weren't entertaining customers.

¼ cup sun-dried tomatoes
½ pound spaghetti
1 tablespoon olive oil
1 medium onion, chopped
2 garlic cloves, minced
8 Italian plum tomatoes, chopped
2 tablespoons capers, with a little juice
¼ cup black olives, sliced
4 anchovy fillets or 1 tablespoon anchovy
    paste (Optional: Don't use if your date is
    a strict vegetarian.)
1 teaspoon oregano
½ teaspoon basil
¼ cup fresh parsley, minced
Freshly ground black pepper and crushed
    red pepper, to taste
Parmesan or Romano cheese, grated

1. Pour ½ cup hot water over the sun-dried tomatoes to let them reconstitute. When they are soft, chop them.

2. Boil water for the pasta. Add spaghetti, cook until al dente and drain.

3. Heat the oil in a large sauté pan. Add the onions and sauté until soft, about 5 minutes. Add the garlic, sun-dried tomatoes, plum tomatoes, capers, olives, anchovy, oregano, basil and parsley. Bring the sauce to a simmer, and cook uncovered, stirring frequently, for a few minutes. Add black and red pepper to taste.

4. Toss sauce with cooked spaghetti and top with cheese.

VEGETARIAN CHILI

This chili is so good that no one will ask "Where's the Beef?" Freeze and defrost the tofu ahead of time for a "meaty" texture.

1 (16 ounce) package firm tofu
1 tablespoon vegetable oil
1 large onion, chopped
2 garlic cloves, minced
1 (28 ounce) can chopped tomatoes with juice
1 (19 ounce) can kidney beans, drained
1 (19 ounce) can black beans, drained
2 tablespoons chili powder
2 teaspoons oregano
1 teaspoon paprika
1 teaspoon sugar
1 tablespoon red wine vinegar
½ teaspoon cayenne pepper
Salt, black pepper and Tabasco sauce, to taste

1. Drain water from tofu, cover with plastic wrap and freeze for several hours. Let tofu thaw at room temperature for 7–8 hours or in the refrigerator for 24 hours before making chili.

2. Heat oil in a large soup or stockpot over medium heat. Sauté the onion until soft, about 5 minutes. Add the garlic and sauté for another 1–2 minutes. Crumble the tofu into the pot and sauté with the garlic and onions for another minute.

3. Add remaining ingredients except the salt, pepper and Tabasco sauce. Cover and simmer, stirring frequently, for about 30 minutes. Add salt, pepper and Tabasco sauce to taste. Dish into bowls, top with sour cream or yogurt, and serve with chips and salsa.

BLACKENED TOFU

Tofu and other soy products can lower cholesterol levels and reduce cancer risk, so we couldn't resist including another tofu recipe. This makes a great sandwich filling or entrée when served with rice.

1 (16 ounce) package firm tofu
1 tablespoon vegetable oil
2 tablespoons blackening seasoning*

1. Heat a large, lightly greased or nonstick skillet over medium-high heat.
2. Cut tofu into eight ½-inch wide, 2-inch high slices. Dip tofu slices into vegetable oil and then into blackening seasoning.
3. Pan fry tofu in preheated skillet for 2–3 minutes per side.

We use Chef Paul Prudhomme's Magic Seasoning Blends.

PYRAMID POTAGE

Cumin, garlic and cayenne pepper give this traditional Egyptian soup a real kick.

    1 tablespoon olive oil
    1 large onion, chopped
    2 garlic cloves, minced
    1 carrot, chopped
    1 teaspoon cumin
    ⅛ teaspoon cayenne pepper, or to taste
    6 cups vegetable stock
    1 (16 ounce) can chickpeas, drained
    1 cup fresh spinach, chopped
    ¼ cup parsley, chopped
    2 tablespoons fresh lemon juice
    Freshly ground black pepper, to taste

1. Heat oil in a large stock or soup pot over medium heat. Add the onion and sauté until soft, about 5 minutes. Add the garlic, carrot, cumin and cayenne pepper. Cook for another 3–4 minutes. (If pan gets dry add a few tablespoons stock.) Add the stock and simmer covered until carrot is soft, about 15–20 minutes.

2. Add the chickpeas, spinach, parsley, lemon juice and pepper. Simmer covered for another 2–3 minutes and serve.

Variation: Add 2 tablespoons fresh, chopped mint leaves in step 2.

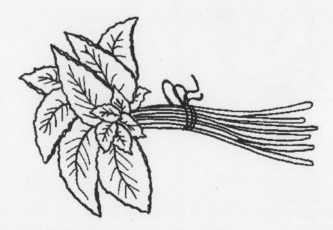

16

Gooey, Drippy, Slurpy

"A dessert course with no cheese is a beauty with only one eye."

— *Brillat-Savarin (the 18th century French gastronome, not the triple creme cheese)*

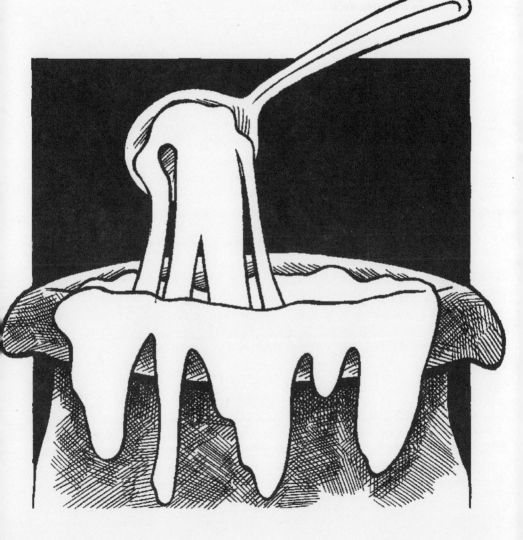

*G*ooey, drippy, slurpy; the name says it all. If you can't figure out what this chapter is about, then you need more than this book to get your love life sizzling and your date/mate salivating.

For our dear readers who have been anxiously awaiting this chapter since they opened the table of contents, we're going to skip the lecture and give you a cheese course instead. So chuck your fork; grab the cheese slicer, a pile of napkins and your sweetheart and get ready to drip, slurp and goo.

CHEESE 101

People have been enjoying cheese for at least 6,000 years. Archeologists speculate potsherds punctured with holes found in Switzerland may have been used to make cheese about 8,000 years ago. Sumerian clay tablets, dating to approximately 4,000 B.C., record cheese production. The Greeks and Romans adored cheese, and so should you. Whether creamy, smooth, robust, sharp or pungent, cheese is a sensual delight.

There are hundreds of different varieties of cheese ready to pleasure your palate. So find a good cheese store that encourages sampling or a restaurant with a cheese course and indulge. Try a new type each week, and soon you'll know cheese from Asiago (great on buttered pasta with black pepper) to Ziger (a whey cheese).

Cheese is usually made by coagulating milk with an acid, so the milk curdles. Then the solids (curds) and liquid (whey) are separated. Next the cheese is processed and aged, which, along with the type of milk used, determines how the cheese will taste. Usually the higher the fat content of the milk, the smoother and richer the cheese. Most cheeses are made from cows', goats' or sheep's milk; but cheese can be made from the milk of lamas, yaks, reindeer, water buffalo, ewe, ass, camel and zebra. Raw milk (which contains its own coagulating bacteria) or processed milk can be used. Cheeses are usually classified by texture (soft, soft-ripened, semisoft, semifirm and firm), type of milk used and place of origin. Here are some of our favorites:

Asiago. A hard cheese with a slight bite.

Bel Paese. A sweet, mild, soft, Italian cheese that does not run like brie or camembert. A great melting cheese, try substituting it for mozzarella in your favorite recipes.

Brie. A soft, smooth, sensual cheese originally from France that oozes when perfectly ripe. Serve with French bread, plain crackers, grapes and white wine, or try our recipe for Baked Brie.

Buffalo mozzarella. A smooth, very mild cheese that's wonderful with a perfectly ripe, sliced tomato and a little basil.

Camembert. Spreadable and brie-like in consistency with a thinner outer shell and a milder flavor. One of our favorites.

Cheddar. Forget boring, prepackaged cheddar. Try tangy, rich Double Gloucester with a glass of port, Canadian Black Diamond with apple slices or a wedge of sharp Vermont with a glass of sparkling cider.

Chèvre (goats' cheese). There are many types of goat cheeses. Flavor varies from pungent and tangy to mild. Goat cheeses tend to get stronger and drier as they age. Available coated with herbs.

Danablu (Danish blue). Invented in 1914 by Marius Boel, who grew the mold for the cheese on a piece of barley bread. This is a creamy, somewhat salty cheese with a strong flavor.

Harvarti. A creamy, semisoft, mild cheese from Denmark that also comes spiked with dill, chives or caraway seeds.

Emmentaler. This cheese has the big holes that will make you think of "Swiss cheese." It has a nutty flavor and is great for melting on sandwiches, over onion soup and in fondue.

Fontina. A very buttery cheese with a nutty flavor that has been made since the 11th century in Lombardy (an Italian town near the Swiss boarder). True Fontina, called Fontina d'Aosta, is expensive and one of the tastiest

THE A,B,C'S OF SERVING CHEESE

Keep your cheese plate simple. Pick three or four different cheeses with contrasting textures, flavors and colors. You may want to start with cheeses from several different countries or select one firm, one semifirm, one soft and one blue-veined cheese.

Serve your selections with bread, crackers (thin, bland crackers are best since they don't mask the flavor of the cheese), fruit and wine and let the cheeses speak for themselves. Serve a few simple wines to see how they interact with the cheeses. Crudités, nuts, olives and interesting condiments, such as chutney or mustard, are other nice additions that you can experiment with.

When choosing cheeses consider what you are making for dinner. If dinner is lavish serve simple cheeses to finish the meal. If dinner is simple splurge on several fabulous, rich cheeses. Consider inviting your date home for a cheese course after a meal out, or serve a few cheeses before dinner as an appetizer.

TREAT YOUR CHEESES RIGHT

Cheese should always be served at room temperature. Soft cheeses take about 45 minutes to come to room temperature; hard cheeses can take a couple hours.

When you're done indulging, wrap cheeses tightly in a fresh piece of plastic wrap or aluminum foil and keep them refrigerated in the dairy or produce drawer. Softer cheeses spoil quickly so make sure to finish that brie or port salute before they deteriorate.

---

cheeses in the world. If you really want to splurge, try it in our recipe for Impromptu Fondue.

Gjestost. Hard to pronounce and rather strange. A semifirm, smooth goat cheese (gjet means "goat" and ost means "cheese") from Norway that reminds us of peanut butter.

Gorgonzola. A green-veined cheese from Italy. Moist, creamy and strong, it gets sharper and drier as it ripens. Serve with walnuts and apples.

Gruyère. From the town of Gruyère, Switzerland, this cheese has a nutty flavor and is great in fondue.

Port Salut. First made by Trappist monks from the abbey of Port-Salut. This is a semisoft cheese with a mild, yet assertive flavor that's great for picnics.

Red Leicester. A bright orange (the color comes from the addition of anatto dye), tangy, crumbly cheese from England that melts into rich creaminess when it hits your mouth. Also great in sauces calling for cheddar.

Saint Andre. A soft, rich, triple creme cheese from France that's great with figs.

Smoked Gouda. This fairly hard cheese has a very attractive smoky, smooth flavor.

Stilton. Serve this pungent, blue-veined cheese with a glass of port in the drawing room.

Valencay. A goats' milk cheese from France with a blue mold skin that has been dusted with charcoal. For the adventurous.

IMPROMPTU FONDUE

We know what you're thinking: Fondue went out with bell bottoms and the Brady Bunch. Well the Bradys are back and bell bottoms are in style, so reconsider this gooey dish. Your mother probably has an old fondue pot in the basement. Steal it. Your mom and dad have been watching their cholesterol levels for over a decade, so you'll be doing them a favor. If your mother doesn't have a fondue pot, use a chaffing dish or double boiler. Once you've discovered fondue, you'll want your own set. Fondue forks are sharp so use them for spearing the bread, not eating. Eat the cheese-dipped morsels with your fingers or a dinner fork. If you don't have a fondue set, you can use bamboo skewers.

A few basic rules to get you started…
1. If the woman loses her bread, she must kiss the man to her right.
2. If the man loses, his bread he must finish his drink.
3. Lose your bread.

1 garlic clove, cut in half
1½ cups dry white wine
4 cups Swiss cheese, grated (about a pound)*
2 tablespoons Kirsch†
1 teaspoon cornstarch
Salt, freshly ground black pepper and paprika, to taste
1 loaf crusty French or Italian bread, cut into bite-size pieces

1. Rub the inside of a saucepan or fondue pot with the garlic clove. Discard clove.

2. Pour in the wine and heat over low burner until air bubbles rise to the surface. Do not boil. Add the cheese, a handful at a time, stirring constantly, letting cheese melt between additions.

3. Mix Kirsch and cornstarch into a smooth paste. When all the cheese has been added and has melted, whisk in the cornstarch mixture. Cook until fondue is thick and creamy, about 2–3 minutes. Season with salt, pepper and paprika.

4. To serve, set fondue pot, chaffing dish or pan over heat source or hot water. Spear bread and dip. If the fondue gets too thick, add a little heated wine. Serve with a simple tossed salad and more wine.

*Cheese Whiz won't do. A mixture of Emmentaler and Gruyère works well.
† Kirsch is the classic flavoring for fondue; however, cognac or applejack also work.

BAKED BRIE

Cheese, glorious cheese. This is one of the greatest ways to enjoy it.

1 cup flour
¼ teaspoon salt
¼ cup butter or margarine, chilled and cut into small pieces
1½ tablespoons vegetable shortening, chilled
2–3 tablespoons ice water
1 (8 ounce) wheel brie
1 egg, beaten with 1 tablespoon water

1. In a food processor mix the flour, salt, butter and vegetable shortening and process in half-second pulses until mixture resembles coarse meal. If you don't have a food processor, combine the flour and salt in a bowl. Add the butter and vegetable shortening and mix with a pastry blender or back of a fork until mixture resembles coarse meal.

2. Sprinkle 2 tablespoons ice water over flour mixture. Using as few strokes as possible, blend mixture with a fork. Using your hands and adding more ice water, a tablespoon at a time only if dough will not stick together, form the dough into a ball. Wrap the dough in plastic and refrigerate for at least 1 hour. (Dough will keep in the refrigerator for 2–3 days and up to a month in the freezer.)

3. Preheat oven to 425°F. Using a lightly floured surface and floured rolling pin, roll out dough until it is approximately ¼-inch thick. Cut one 5-inch circle and one 7-inch circle. Place the 5-inch circle on a greased baking sheet and center the brie on top. Brush the boarder of the pastry, from cheese to cut edge, with beaten egg. Center the 7-inch circle on top of the brie. Fold the dough over the brie and press into the smaller circle of dough completely sealing the brie in pastry. Cut away any excess dough. Using moistened fingers, smooth dough around brie. (You can form the pastry around the brie a few hours before you plan to serve it, cover and keep refrigerated until ready to bake.)

4. Brush pastry with beaten egg. Bake until golden brown, about 20 minutes.

MÉNAGE À TROIS SOUP GRATINÉ

A twist on a French classic that's perfect for a moody Monday or an elegant, slurpy supper.

  3 tablespoons butter
  3 large onions, thinly sliced
  1 cup peeled sliced shallots
  1 tablespoon sugar
  3 cups sliced mushrooms (about 3/4 pound)
  6 cups beef broth
  ¼ teaspoon freshly ground black pepper
  ½ cup Gruyère cheese, grated
  2 (1-inch thick) slices French bread, toasted

1. In a large stockpot melt butter over medium-low heat. Add onions, shallots and sugar. Cover and cook, stirring occasionally, until onions and shallots are wilted, about 15 minutes.

2. Add mushrooms and sauté for 1–2 minutes. Add beef stock, cover and simmer for 20 minutes.

3. Preheat broiler. Ladle soup into oven-proof or onion soup bowls. Place toasted bread on top, cover with grated Gruyère cheese. Place under the broiler and cook until cheese is melted and bubbly.

17

Caribbean Blue

"Just thoughts, funny thoughts about you
and me."
— *Brooke Shields, in the film* Blue Lagoon

Y ou're lying with your lover on a pillow of sand, the sky's an azure sea. The ocean creeps closer, licking your toes while you nuzzle your sweetheart. The warm, clear, blue water inches closer; foamy kisses lick your body. *From Here to Eternity* becomes a reality, and you understand why Burt Lancaster and Deborah Kerr stayed on that beach all night. Another wave washes over you as your lips meet and…

Nothing heats up romance like love on the beach especially if the beach is on an enchanted Caribbean island. Silky sunsets, velvet heat, cool passionate nights, long lazy days, everything is a celebration. If you can't get to Tobago, Saint Bart's or Montego Bay, bring the islands to Kansas City, Saint Paul or Sheepshead Bay — wherever you call home.

Shut out winter, banish the weatherman. Draw the curtains, crank the heat up to 75° and dump those Christmas decorations. Put on that Hawaiian shirt or sexy little sun dress. Plant a hibiscus behind your right ear (it means you're single) and dig out the Hawaiian lei you saved from one of those freshman frat parties. Then ask yourself: "Why did I save this thing?"

It's time for hot steel drums, Bob Marley and a samba. Kick off your shoes, push the furniture aside and boogie until the sweat pours down your bodies and you slide through each other's arms like butter dancing on a sizzling hot skillet.

Take out the blender and, presto, a batch of pina coladas magically appears. Too early? Nonsense, in the Caribbean summer and happy hour are endless. The bikinis go on at 8:00 a.m. and the bar opens at 9. So pass the tanning butter and enjoy. When the coladas are gone, mix up a batch of rum punch.

Feeling adventurous? Buy a fresh coconut with milk. (When you're at the store, shake the coconuts. Yes, people will look at you funny. If your nut makes

Do the Samba: This light little dance hails from Brazil. Keep your body loose and get ready for a real workout. The basic rhythm (for those of you who aspire to be Fred and Ginger) is slow, quick, slow. You can move forward, backward or flop onto the couch.

Once you've mastered the samba, why not try a rumba, mambo or tango? Just listen to the bongo and follow the dancing feet.

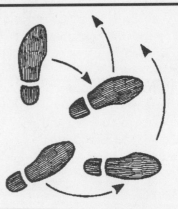

RUM RUNNERS

You don't have to go on a rum runner cruise to enjoy this classic Caribbean punch.

1 cup orange juice
1 cup pineapple juice
1 cup ginger ale
1 tablespoon lemon or lime juice
1 tablespoon grenadine
1/2 cup dark rum

Lemon, lime, orange or pineapple slices, for garnish

Combine orange juice, pineapple juice, ginger ale, lemon or lime juice, grenadine and rum in a small pitcher. Serve over ice and garnish with lemon, lime, orange or pineapple slices.

---

a sloshing noise it's full of milk.) Next, impress your date by opening your coconut like a native. Power tools work great, but there's more than one way to crack this nut. You can punch holes where you see three black dots at the top with a sharp screwdriver and hammer. You can also heat the coconut in a 325°F oven for 15 minutes (don't overcook), wrap in a cloth and hit lightly with a hammer to crack the shell. (This method is messier and doesn't look as cool.) Drain the milk and mix ⅓ cup with 1 shot rum and 1 teaspoon sugar. Pour over ⅔ cup crushed ice, then mix in a scoop of vanilla ice cream or frozen yogurt. If you really want to get fancy, serve the drinks in one half of the coconut shell and garnish with a miniature umbrella or a maraschino cherry. We call this concoction "Coconut Cool Aid." Drink enough of these and you'll forget what cold is. If your coconut has dried up or all you can find is grated coconut meat, mix 1 cup unsweetened grated coconut with 1 cup hot water in a blender. Let sit for 30 minutes, strain through a sieve and use like fresh coconut milk. In a pinch you can buy canned, unsweetened coconut milk at the supermarket.

Your simulated beach party is set; now it's time for love. Sex on a simulated beach has advantages. No sunburn, no bugs, no natives, no unwelcome strangers, no sharks and no sand in your hair and you know where. Spread that beach blanket and dive into the evening. Grab the massage oil and rub away winter aches. Watch *Beach Blanket Bingo, Gidget Goes Hawaiian* or any Elvis movie, and you're in the mood. Pretend you're Frankie and Annette, and decide for yourselves whether they really "did it."

By now, your head should be spinning and your appetite callin'. Keep the heat on high with our hot and spicy Caribe menu. Fill the air with zouk, reggae, curry and salsa, whip up a batch of Hot Chops or Reggae Bouillabaisse and let the party begin.

REGGAE BOUILLABAISSE

Here's our Caribbean version of this classic French fish stew.

2 tablespoons vegetable oil
1 large onion, chopped
1 garlic clove, minced
1 tablespoon gingerroot, finely chopped
½ green bell pepper, diced
½ red bell pepper, diced
½ jalapeno pepper, minced
¾ cup white wine
2 tablespoons Pernod, a licorice flavored liqueur
½ teaspoon fennel seeds
2 tablespoons fresh parsley, minced
Pinch of saffron
½ pound boneless white fish (such as monkfish haddock, cod or
    snapper), cut into 1½-inch chunks
1 pound mussels, scrubbed and debearded
½ pound shrimp, peeled and deveined
¼ cup lime juice
Salt and freshly ground black pepper, to taste

1. Heat the oil in a large soup pot. Add the onion and sauté until soft, about 5 minutes. Add the garlic, gingerroot, bell and jalapeno peppers and cook for another 1–2 minutes.

2. Stir in the wine, Pernod, fennel seeds, parsley, saffron and ½ cup water. Bring to a boil, lower the heat and simmer covered for 15 minutes.

3. Add the white fish and simmer uncovered until fish is opaque, 3–5 minutes. Add the mussels and simmer covered for another 3–5 minutes. Add the shrimp and simmer covered until shrimp are opaque and mussels are open. Add the lime juice, salt and pepper to taste. Serve in bowls with French bread.

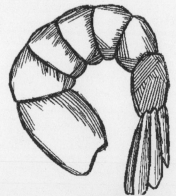

JAMAICAN JERK CHICKEN

This recipe also works well on pork tenderloin. Serve with grilled vegetables, plain rice and cool bottles of lager beer.

2 bunches scallions, chopped (mostly the white with a little of the green)
2 tablespoons olive oil
½ cup orange juice
¼ cup lemon juice
2 tablespoons lime juice
¼ cup soy sauce
1 tablespoon peeled fresh gingerroot, minced
1 tablespoon fresh thyme leaves
1 teaspoon ground coriander
1 teaspoon allspice
1 teaspoon cinnamon
1 teaspoon ground nutmeg
½–1 jalapeno or Scotch bonnet pepper
  (depending on how spicy you want
  your chicken)
1 teaspoon freshly ground black pepper
1 chicken, cut into quarters

1. Combine all the ingredients except chicken, in a food processor or blender and purée until smooth. If you don't have a food processor, mix ingredients well by hand. Rub mixture over chicken pieces and place in a large covered bowl or glass dish. Let marinate, turning pieces occasionally, for at least 4 hours or overnight.

2. Light the grill. Grill the chicken over medium-hot fire, turning pieces occasionally until juices run clear when chicken thigh is pierced with a fork, about 15 minutes per side. Serve hot.

HOT CHOPS

This recipe is so spicy that it will smoke up your kitchen, so keep the windows open and stand back while you cook. Serve chops with Coconut Rice or sweet potatoes.

½ teaspoon cayenne pepper
½ teaspoon curry powder
½ teaspoon cumin
½ teaspoon powdered ginger
½ tablespoon course salt (Kosher or sea salt)
½ teaspoon freshly ground white pepper
½ teaspoon freshly ground black pepper
1–1½ pounds pork chops (1–2 chops per a person)
1 tablespoon vegetable oil
Mango chutney

1. In a small dish combine cayenne pepper, curry powder, cumin, ginger, salt, black pepper and white pepper.
2. Heat a large cast-iron skillet over medium heat.
3. Brush the pork chops with the vegetable oil, and sprinkle with some of the spice mixture. The more you use the hotter the chops will be.
4. When skillet is hot, pan-fry the pork chops until done, turning a few times, about 10 minutes per side. Serve immediately with mango chutney.

COCONUT RICE

A simple way to add flair to plain boiled rice.

½ cup unsweetened coconut, grated
1 cup unsweetened coconut milk
1 cup water
½ teaspoon salt
1 cup white rice
1 bunch scallions, white only, sliced

1. Toast the coconut by baking in a 350°F oven until light brown, about 12 minutes.
2. In a medium saucepan, combine the coconut milk, water and salt. Bring to a boil. Add rice, stir with a fork, reduce heat to low, cover and cook until the rice is tender, about 15–20 minutes. Remove the rice from the heat and let stand 5 minutes. Stir in the toasted coconut and chopped scallions and serve.

18

Lobster Love Affair

"Bait the hook well: this fish will bite."
— *William Shakespeare*

*W*hat is it about those crazy little things called crustaceans? Sucking succulent lobster meat from the shell transforms the odd couple into the hot couple. If you're already hot, watch out! Remember Woody Allen and Diane Keaton in *Annie Hall* trying to tackle a pair of crustaceans threatening to take over their apartment? We may not be as funny as Woody, but you won't need a tennis racket to subdue dinner with our lobster recipes.

Our first lobster love affair occurred in the summer of '92. The day was perfect, hot, not humid, and I had a date with a tough-looking guy from Brooklyn who kissed like Warren Beatty, and cooked like a dream. Michael picked me up in his red Triumph convertible at 3:00 p.m. The top was down, mine was still up. We were primed for fun and romance.

> *"Where to?" he asked.*
> *"The beach," I said.*

Off on another adventure. Two crazy kids deeply in lust with nothing but miles of road and sunshine ahead. Of course, I should have packed a marvelous picnic to seduce Michael and satisfy our hunger, but the concept of using food as foreplay hadn't occurred to me yet. I didn't worry about food. I was too busy fixing my hair and doing my nails to fix sandwiches and bake cookies. We were destined to starve.

By the time we hit the beach, most folks were heading home. We had the

---

SEE 'EM SWIM

Lobsters usually have two claws — the larger one's for cracking mollusks; the smaller, sharper one's for shredding fish — two pairs of antennae and four pairs of little legs.

You can determine a lobster's sex from the feathery appendages that run under the tail. The set furthest away from the end of the tail is soft for females and hard for males. Some people swear that the meat from female lobsters is more tender, but we really can't tell the difference.

When shopping for live lobsters you can ignore the sex, but look for lobsters that are active. Lively lobsters have probably spent less time in the tank and are still fat. (Lobsters often stop eating in captivity and lose weight.) Buy one large lobster to share (about 3 pounds) or two smaller lobsters (1–1 1/2 pounds).

Almost every part of a lobster is edible except for the vein (which runs along the tail), the gills and the head sac (which is actually the stomach). Whatever else you can suck or pick out is yours for the eating including the liver (the green stuff called tomalley) and the roe (the red stuff).

HOW TO EAT A LOBSTER

1. Don't name your lobster. It makes it hard to enjoy dinner.
2. Turn your lobster over on to its back, and with a large knife make a slit from the head to the tail. Using a towel, to keep from burning yourself, hold both sides of the body and break the lobster apart. The tail meat should now be free. (Be sure to remove the black vein before eating the tail.)
3. Now rip off the claws. Pull the small hinged piece of the claw off and then, using a nutcracker or small hammer, crack the large section of the claw. Peel away the shell and free the meat.
4. Once you've devoured the tail and claws, you'll probably want more. Remove the legs, one at a time, and suck out the meat. Finally, get a small seafood fork or toothpick and scavenge for any morsels that you missed. The harder you work the sweeter the meat.

---

sea to ourselves. Day disappeared and so did our clothes as we swam under the fading sun. We watched the sunset, serenaded by grumbling stomachs, as our appetites emerged. Famished, we searched for food. The snack bar was closed, the Good Humor Man was no where in sight and all we had was a pack of Wrigley Spearmint Gum. (Where is the Ice Cream Man when you need him? Why isn't there a 911 number for hungry people? How much gum do you need to chew to get full? Hey, we want answers to these questions.)

We checked clam shacks, seafood shanties and fried fish emporiums, but most restaurants were packed. The ones that weren't smelled like gynecological experiments gone berserk.

"Let's pick up lobsters," Michael suggested.

He shifted into fifth, and 10 minutes later we were in Sam's Lobster Pound auditioning crustaceans for a starring role in The Dinner. We picked two frisky lobsters to match our mood. On the way to my apartment, we stopped at Lucy's Roadside Farm Stand for corn, bread, butter, and strawberries. (Ricky, Fred and Ethel were nowhere in sight.)

Hoping our day at the beach would lead to a romantic evening, I had planned ahead. A bottle of wine was chilling in the fridge in case things heated up when we got home. After we arrived at my apartment, I uncorked the wine and started boiling water. Michael concocted his special "Death's Head Garlic Bread" and sang *Born To Run,* loud and off key. When a man kisses like Warren Beatty, you ignore the little eccentricities.

On went the jazz, off came our shoes and out we went to watch the stars.

Suddenly our appetites shifted. We were hungry for romance. The lobsters rustling in their bag reminded us that a delicious dinner was moments away. We stashed them in the fridge, turned down the water and turned up the stereo. I opened a bag of Japanese peanut crackers, Michael poured two glasses of wine, and we toasted the night under the moonlight. The lobsters could wait, we couldn't.

BOILED OR STEAMED LOBSTER

The simplest ways to cook lobster. Both methods work well although boiling is a little faster.

2 (1–2 pound) lobsters
Salt

1. For boiled lobster fill a pot, larger than the lobsters, ¾ of the way with salted water (1 tablespoon per quart of water). For steamed lobster place a steaming rack in the bottom of the pot and fill with 2 inches salted water. Bring water to a boil. When water boils throw the lobsters in, head first, cover and flee. When the water comes back to a boil set the timer and the table. One to two pound lobsters cook in about 7–10 minutes, after the water starts boiling again, via the boiling method and 9–12 minutes via the steaming method.

2. Remove the lobsters from the pot and let them cool until you can handle them without burning your fingers. Heed this rule of burnt thumb: Dates can't be too hot, lobsters can. Trust us, these little babies *will* get their revenge even after death. Lobster should be eaten with your hands and served in the shell accompanied by lemon and melted butter. If you need a lesson on how to eat lobster, read our side bar "How to Eat a Lobster," rent *Flash Dance* or dig in and figure it out as you go. Eating lobster is the most fun mess you're ever gonna have.

GRILLED LOBSTER

This method is not for the faint of heart, but it is delicious.

2 (1–2 pound) lobsters
Vegetable oil
Garlic or Basil Butter or plain butter, melted (Recipes follow. We like fresh,
    chopped basil with a pinch of cayenne pepper for this recipe.)
Salt and freshly ground black pepper, to taste

1. Fire up the grill and set the heat at medium.
2. Place live lobster on its back on a cutting board. To sever the spinal
vein, stab the lobster through the mouth at the cross-shaped mark behind the
head with a sharp, heavy knife. (You can ask the nice person at the fish store
to do this for you, or you can boil the lobster for 4 minutes and then grill it,
making sure to reduce cooking time by 1–2 minutes per side.)
3. With a heavy cleaver or knife, split the lobster in half lengthwise.
Remove and discard the intestinal vein in the tail and the head sack behind
the eyes. Crack the top of the claws and separate them from the body. (Steps 2
and 3 can be done a few hours before you're ready to cook the lobsters.)
4. When the grill is hot and you're ready to eat, brush the lobster meat,
claws and shell with vegetable oil and sprinkle with salt and pepper. Brush the
underside of the lobster and claws with Garlic or Basil Butter or plain butter.
Place claws and lobster, flesh side down on the grill, cover grill, and cook for
about 2–3 minutes. Flip over and brush the meat with more flavored or plain
butter. Cook until flesh is firm and opaque, about 4–5 minutes.

FLAVORED BUTTERS

Flavored butters are great on everything from vegetables (especially corn) to steak and seafood.

HERB BUTTER

½ cup butter, allowed to soften at room temperature
3 tablespoons herbs, chopped
2 teaspoons lemon juice
Salt and freshly ground pepper, to taste

1. Combine butter with chopped herbs and lemon juice. Add salt and pepper to taste. Chill until ready to use.

GARLIC BUTTER

½ cup butter, allowed to soften at room temperature
2 garlic cloves, pressed
2 teaspoons lemon juice
Salt and freshly ground pepper, to taste

1. Combine the butter with garlic and lemon juice. Add salt and pepper, to taste. Chill until ready to use.

CHILI BUTTER

½ cup butter, allowed to soften at room temperature
1 tablespoon chili powder
Salt and freshly ground pepper, to taste

1. Combine the butter with the chili powder. Add salt and pepper to taste. Chill until ready to use.

CORN

Corn on the cob should be eaten as fresh as possible (preferably the day you buy it) because the sugar in corn starts turning into starch after the corn is picked. Fresh corn is generally available in early July. Buy it locally, if possible, at a farm stand right next to the cornfield. Look for heavy ears with small moist kernels. Store corn, with the husks on, in a plastic bag in the refrigerator. When ready to cook the corn, remove husks and silk and pop ears in lightly salted boiling water, cover and return to a boil.

> *"OUCH! The corn ears, Ellen."*
> *"Sorry honey. Come here, I'll put some ice on them. Poor baby."*
> *"How come I always get hurt in the chapters you write alone?"*
> *"Coincidence?"*

Cook until tender, about 5 minutes. For a real taste treat, find a friend or friendly farmer with a cornfield, start the water boiling, run out and pick several ears and drop them right into the pot.

For roasted or grilled corn remove the silk, peel back husks, leaving them attached at the top, and soak the husks in water for about 15 minutes. Pull the husks back around the corn and twist or tie shut. Grill or roast for about 15 minutes turning frequently. Whatever method you use serve with plenty of butter (regular or flavored), salt and pepper.

19

The Perfect Picnic

"A Jug of Wine, a Loaf of Bread and Thou."
— *Edward FitzGerald*

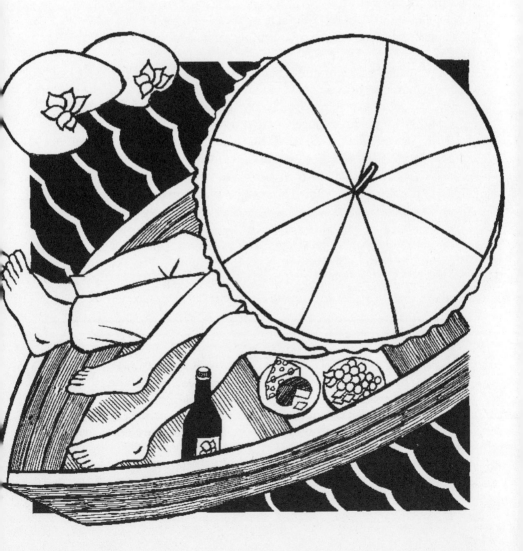

*I*n spring, thoughts turn from frozen feet and the flu to flowers and romance. The birds and bees know what to do, what about YOU? Put away your sweaters and pull out a T-shirt. Tint your hair red? Ah…maybe not. Rent a convertible for the weekend? *Definitely!* Pack a picnic and drive into the sunset.

We're not talking greasy piles of fried chicken and stale chips stuffed into an old shoe box. We're talking class: brie and chablis. Poached lobster, herb rolls, Caesar salad and imported beer. Hummus, stuffed grape leaves and ambrosia. Got the idea? Ordinary sandwiches? Hell no, *extraordinary* sandwiches. Smoked salmon and boursin on focaccia. Turkey with cranberry chutney on corn bread.

Sound good? You bet. Your date will think you spent the day cooking. Not a chance, 'cause you're too busy planning romance. Forget the kitchen. The perfect picnic starts with you.

If you don't have a mountain or beach around, visit the park or schedule a midnight rendezvous on the veranda. Eat under the stars while the world sleeps and your heart skips a beat. Wake at dawn for a sunrise picnic. Take three hours for lunch and meet at the zoo. (Attempt this one only if you've recently broken all sales records at your company.) Don't forget peanuts for Jumbo and Cracker Jacks for the two of you. Check the paper for outdoor concerts. Sneak off to a lake and dine in a canoe or rubber raft. Remember, spikes and rubber rafts don't mix. Trust us on this one, experience counts. Leave the shoes on shore! Besides, it's a great excuse to have him carry you to and from the boat. Pretend to cruise the canals of Venice. Just don't stand up. Bring your guitar and serenade your sweetheart with an aria, or read Shakespearean love sonnets to each other.

Make sure to pack food for travel. Pull out the Tupperware Aunt Ethel gave you for Christmas. Wrap sandwiches in extra foil and don't sit on the

---

OUR PERFECT PICNIC

Date: May 28, 1995
Time: 11:30 a.m
Place: An open field near the
junction of Weston & Lincoln
Roads, Lincoln, Massachusetts
Menu:
- Assorted bagels with lox, cream cheese and red onions
- Feta and Seafood Pasta Salad
- Strawberries dipped in sour cream and brown sugar
- Brownies
- Franciscan Barrel Fermented Oakville Estate Nappa Valley Chardonnay 1993
- Iced cappuccino

"TOO FEW PEOPLE UNDERSTAND A REALLY GOOD SANDWICH"—JAMES BEARD

Classic sandwiches (roast beef, ham & cheese, tuna, turkey) are fine during the week, but when you're on a picnic you want a special combination. Here are some of our favorites:

- Smoked salmon with cream cheese, sliced cucumber and red onion
- Avocado with herb cheese and sprouts
- Harvarti and munster cheese with pesto and sliced tomato or roasted red peppers
- Salsa, guacamole and cheddar
- Smoked turkey with havarti and scallions
- Turkey with bacon and avocado
- Black Forest ham with brie and honey mustard
- Prosciutto with Aioli, mozzarella and tomato
- Grilled tuna with roasted red peppers, red onions and mozzarella
- Crumbled feta cheese, chopped olives, chopped basil, tomatoes and spinach in a pita pocket with vinaigrette dressing
- Hummus, tomato, cucumber, black olives, red onion and sprouts

Of course never rule out PB&J (peanut butter and jelly). You can make it special by adding raisins, honey, sliced bananas or sliced apples.

Don't forget to buy good bread that suits your filling. This means no Wonder stuff! Try seven grain, lavish, focaccia, French, challah, anadama, pumpernickel or sour dough. And experiment with condiments. Try a flavored mustard or make your own by mixing herbs, lemon or lime juice, honey or grated horseradish, to taste with a little Dijon mustard. You can spice up mayonnaise with herbs, garlic or curry powder, to taste. And salsa or chutney are also great on sandwiches.

cookies. Freeze a juice box or portable ice pack to keep food cold, and if it's a hot day and you're driving, keep food up front with you and not in the trunk where it can get overheated. You don't want to consummate your love with salmonella. To avoid getting burned or bitten, don't forget sunscreen and bug repellent. Throw a citronella candle in for good measure.

Food can be made a day ahead and chilled (this also helps flavors develop). Lazy? Busy? Pick up fancy sandwich fixings or marinated salads at a deli or gourmet shop on the way. Keep the menu simple and don't forget champagne, wine, good beer (this means no Bud, bud) or sparkling cider (great with sharp cheddar and multi-grain bread). Wrap the bottle in wet newspaper to keep it cold. Honest, it works.

If it rains don't complain. Spread a blanket on the living room floor, listen to the drops dance on the roof and recline in your best Cleopatra pose while he feeds you peeled grapes and Shrimp Arabesque.

Ever consider a hotel picnic? Pack a bag of essentials and a picnic supper (the food should take up a lot more room than your clothes). Check into your favorite hotel and then tell your date that the two of you are going out to eat, and surprise your lover with a room key and a bib. This is one meal where someone else gets to clean the crumbs out of the bed. If you really want to splurge (especially for birthdays, anniversaries and marriage proposals), spring for plane tickets, pack a bag for your mate and jet your lover away to another city for a weekend long hotel picnic. Add concert or theater tickets in your destination city, and you have all the makings for a weekend to be remembered.

Don't forget, picnics should be *fun*. So don't spend a lot of time in the kitchen. You should be out enjoying yourself. The perfect picnic starts with you.

PESTO STUFFED CHICKEN BREASTS

These juicy chicken breasts take only about 15 minutes to prepare and are wonderful hot or cold. The garlicky pesto filling contrasts nicely with the chicken.

½ cup almonds, chopped
¼ cup bread crumbs
¼ cup Parmesan cheese, grated
4 skinless, boneless chicken breast halves
¼ cup pesto (recipe follows)
Salt and freshly ground pepper, to taste
Olive oil

1. Combine the chopped almonds, bread crumbs and Parmesan cheese on a plate.

2. Place the chicken breasts between waxed paper and pound with mallet or cleaver to ¼-inch thickness. Sprinkle the chicken with salt and pepper. Place 1 tablespoon pesto at the narrow end of each chicken breast. Starting on the long side, roll up each chicken breast. Brush with olive oil and dip in the nut and bread crumb mixture.

3. Place the chicken rolls, seam side down, in an oiled baking pan. (Chicken can be prepared, covered and refrigerated 8 hours ahead.) Bake at 350°F until coating is crisp and chicken is cooked through, about 30 minutes.

PESTO

Keep pesto on hand to spread on bread, toss with pasta or add to soups.

¼ cup olive oil
2 garlic cloves
½ cup Parmesan cheese, grated
3 cups fresh basil leaves
½ cup fresh parsley leaves
½ cup walnuts or pine nuts

1. Place all the ingredients in a food processor or blender and process until smooth. Cover the pesto with a thin layer of olive oil, store in an airtight container in the refrigerator and it will keep for several weeks.

HUMMUS

Hummus is practically a staple for us. We use it as a sandwich spread, a dip and a sauce for steamed vegetables.

1 (15–16 ounce) can chickpeas
¼ cup sesame tahini
1 garlic clove
3 tablespoons lemon juice
Salt, black pepper and cayenne pepper, to taste

1. Place all the ingredients in a food processor or blender and process until smooth. Add enough water (or additional lemon juice if you like very lemony hummus) to make a thin paste. Chill until ready to serve.

SPICY PEANUT NOODLES

Bring a touch of the Orient to your next picnic. If you can't stand the heat, be careful with the hot chili oil or Tabasco sauce. For a mellower dish add only a dash.

½ teaspoon gingerroot, grated

2 tablespoons dark sesame oil

3 tablespoons soy sauce

2 tablespoons rice vinegar

½ cup peanut butter

½ cup strong brewed tea

1 tablespoon honey

½–1 teaspoon Tabasco sauce or hot chili oil*

8 ounces soba noodles* or linguine

2 scallions, finely chopped

2 cups bean sprouts

2 tablespoons unsalted roasted peanuts

1. Combine the gingerroot, sesame oil, soy sauce, vinegar, peanut butter, tea, honey and Tabasco sauce or hot chili oil. Mix until smooth.

2. Cook the noodles until al dente, drain and toss with sauce. Chill for several hours or overnight.

3. When ready to serve top with scallions, bean sprouts and peanuts. This is best served at room temperature.

Soba (Japanese-style buckwheat noodles) and hot chili oil are available in Asian markets and natural food stores.

JAPANESE SLAW

A new, low-fat twist on the coleslaw theme. Arame, a nutty, sweet sea vegetable, adds flavor and an interesting texture.

¼ cup arame*
4 cups sliced red cabbage
2 teaspoons sesame seeds
¼ cup rice vinegar*
2 tablespoons soy sauce
1 tablespoon mirin* or sake
1 teaspoon sugar

1. Wash the arame by submerging in cold water and swirling to remove sand and dirt. Place the arame in a bowl, cover with water and soak for 30 minutes to rehydrate.

2. Steam the red cabbage by placing in a steamer basket over boiling water and cooking for 2–3 minutes.

3. Toast the sesame seeds at 350°F until golden brown, about 5 minutes. (Watch carefully so they don't burn.)

4. For the dressing, mix the soy sauce, rice vinegar, mirin or sake and sugar. Toss the cabbage and arame in a bowl, cover with the dressing and sprinkle with sesame seeds. Refrigerate for at least an hour to let flavors blend.

Arame, rice vinegar and mirin (a sweet Japanese cooking wine) are available in natural food stores and Asian markets.

20

Slave to Love

"Know, my love, that I should like to call you a thief, because you have stolen my heart."

— *Margaret of Nassau*

*A*t last they're yours, the keys to your lover's apartment. It took weeks of wining, dining and whining, hours on the phone and a small fortune in flowers to win your sweetheart over. Now it's time to capture your love — body, heart and soul. You need to set the trap. Succeed and you will be remembered as one of the world's greatest lovers (well, at least in your mate's eyes).

Inscribe the date you want to capture your lover in your heart and on your Day Runner, so you can plot the plan. We've sketched out several menu possibilities to help out, but you'll want to cater the affair to your date's specs. Would your love rather have a bubble bath or a deep muscle massage? (We'd opt for both, but then again it's our book.) Would a meal made of chocolate turn your honey on? Would your hunk or hunkette rather eat steak and potatoes? Does your Don Juan hate fish but love baby carrots sautéed in butter? If you don't know it's definitely too early in the game to play capture the lover. Turn to Chapter 4, "Getting to Know You"; you're still in early courting mode. Start asking questions and get better acquainted.

To ensure the perfect evening, give yourself plenty of time to set your trap. You don't want to be scrambling at the last minute. Tell your lover you've caught the flu and can't see him/her until the end of the week.

Our sizzling supper ideas can be bought several days in advance and assembled the night before the big date. For appetizers buy a pound of cooked shrimp with cocktail sauce and a round of brie with crackers. For the main course we suggest Salmon Teriyaki with rice pilaf and asparagus. If you don't have time to make our marinade, purchase a bottle of teriyaki sauce for the fish. Buy a box of rice pilaf and a pound of asparagus. (Snap off the woody ends and scrub the asparagus stalks in advance. Right before serving dinner, cook the asparagus in boiling water for about 5 minutes and drizzle with lemon juice and melted butter.) Other easy, sexy menu options include Shrimp Arabesque and Simple Sensation Steak.

On the big day skip out of work early. Tell your boss that the sister you haven't seen in three years is flying in from Europe and you're picking her up at the airport. Haven't got a sister? Lie. Stop at the store for anything you forgot to buy during the week. A fresh loaf of bread is always a nice touch. Imagine ripping it apart, smothering it with butter and indulging until only crumbs are left.

Get home and pamper yourself before sneaking into your lover's pad. Shave, wax, manicure, puff, buff, scrub, dye, apply and remove whatever to look great. Iron the sexiest outfit you have. Gorgeous? Call your date's apartment to make sure no one is home and don't leave a message. If all is clear, pack up your food in a cooler, stash your stuff in a garment bag, get in your car and drive. (If you don't have a car, treat yourself to a cab. This is no time to be shlepping on buses and subways.) Remember, park down the block where your lover won't see your car (Detective Fiction 101). We hope there's no doorman and the dog's gotten used to you. If not, slip the doorman a ten (if you live in New York or L.A., make it a twenty) and the pooch a box of Milk Bones (in New York or L.A., make it sirloin).

You've got two hours until your lover arrives tired and grouchy after another horrible day at the office. Your job is total transformation. Succeed and you may have captured a mate for life. Start by setting the table. If your date doesn't have nice china, visit Crate & Barrel and treat your honey to a set or bring your own dishes. Don't forget a table cloth or place mats, napkins, cutlery, flowers and champagne. Buy a pair of champagne glasses and present them to your lover as a memento of this fabulous evening together. When the table is set, do any last minute preparation and lay out the cheese and crackers.

Nervous? Your love will be here in under an hour. Calm down, take a break and bake cookies. Wonderful smells are an important part of the trap and the cookies will perfume the air. (Remember this tip in 10 years when the two of you are trying to sell your starter house.) Chocolate chip cookies are the definitive homey smell. Your date's mouth will start to water like a Pavlovian dog trapped in a bell tower. Forget baking them from scratch, you don't have the time. Buy refrigerated cookie dough. Stop it! Don't eat the raw dough, it's tacky. Besides, you should be saving your appetite for romance. Okay, go ahead, but just a little.

Thirty minutes and counting. (Or should we say courting?) Get dressed or undressed. It all depends on what stage the relationship is. Don't forget to take the cookies out of the oven. Ten minutes to go. Close the blinds, dim the lights, turn on soft music, run a bath. Make it on the hot side and close the bathroom door so it will be the right temperature for later. Five minutes left.

ROMANTIC HARMONIES

We suggest Joe Henderson, Frank Morgan or Billie Holiday. Some other great selections are:

Robbie Robertson, "Storyville"
Graham Parker, "The Graham Parker Anthology, Passion Is No Ordinary Word"

Enigma, "M C M X C a. D."
Various artists, "Hitsville USA, The Motown Singles Collection" to really get your feet movin'
Miles Davis, "Ballads"
Duke Ellington, "New Orleans Suite"

THE PERFECT BATH

Whether you own a plain old tub (first invented in 1700 B.C. in Crete) or a fancy jacuzzi, baths are a luxury that few of us indulge in enough. Sure, showering together is fun, but why not indulge in a hot soak? You don't have to stand up, and it's easier to soap and play. Just don't let the water overflow and flood the guy living in the apartment beneath you. He may call the super and blow your whole evening.

For the perfect bath, keep the water around body temperature (96-98°F). Use an inflatable bath pillow or rolled towels to cushion your head. Light scented candles and provide plush, clean towels, hot from the dryer.

For a refreshing summer bath, add 1 cup of lemon juice to the water. For a beauty bath, à la Cleopatra, add 1 quart milk or 1 cup powdered milk to the tub. For a kiddie bath reach for Mr. Bubbles and splash away.

If these ideas don't appeal to you, visit your local health and beauty store for a wonderful selection of scented bath oils, beads and soaps. When bathing together don't forget a back scrubber, grapes and champagne.

Pour yourself a glass of wine, put on Roxy Music or Rachmahnanov, whatever fits your mood. Relax, try to still your heart and not spill your drink.

Watch as your honey bunch comes up the street. Listen as your lover climbs the stairs, walks down the hall, fumbles for keys and opens the door. Greet your sweetheart with a smile, a glass of wine and a plate of cookies. The foundation has been laid for a fabulous evening. Take your date's briefcase and whatever else moves you. Lead your sweetie into the living room and silently take a spin across the dance floor. While you're dancing undo your lover's buttons one by one or slowly unzip whatever needs unzipping. By the time the waltz is over, the two of you will be naked and ready for that hot bath. Play, splash, make love. When you're done towel each other off. Wrap your lover in a soft robe, lead your sweetheart to the dinner table and serve. Cherries jubilee won't be necessary. You are dessert!

SALMON TERIYAKI

Try serving this dish with plain white rice and our recipe for Japanese Slaw.

½ cup sake
2 tablespoons rice or white wine vinegar
¼ cup soy sauce
1 tablespoon toasted sesame oil
1 teaspoon gingerroot, grated
2 tablespoons honey
1–1½ pounds salmon steaks (2, 8–12 ounce steaks)
2 tablespoons sesame seeds, toasted

1. In a small bowl mix the sake, vinegar, soy sauce, sesame oil, gingerroot and honey.
2. Pour over the fish and marinate for about an hour.
3. Preheat the broiler. Place the fish in an oiled baking dish and pour the marinade over the fish. Broil fish 3–4 inches from the heat, flipping once and basting with marinade, until fish is opaque, about 8 minutes total per inch. Watch fish carefully: Thinner steaks may need only 3 minutes per side, while thicker steaks may need 5 minutes per side.
4. Sprinkle with toasted sesame seeds and serve with rice.

SIMPLE SENSATION STEAK

Dinner doesn't get much easier than this. Serve steak with Broiled Tomatoes or a salad and Crispy Cheese Potatoes or French bread.

1 (8 ounce) bottle Italian salad dressing
1 London broil steak (1–1½ pounds)

1. Place the steak in a glass or plastic baking dish or bowl. Pour the dressing over the steak and allow to marinate for 4–24 hours, the longer the better.
2. Preheat the grill. Remove the steak from the dressing and grill to desired doneness, flipping once. (A 2-inch steak done medium-rare takes 10–15 minutes per side.) You can also broil the steak by placing it 3–4 inches from the heat source and cooking 4 minutes per side. Make sure to cook the steak on the rare side or it will be tough.
3. Slice thinly across the grain and serve.

CRISPY CHEESE POTATOES

Prepare these before cooking the steak, and let warm on the bottom rack of the oven while the steak is cooking.

> Vegetable oil or cooking spray
> 3 medium baking potatoes (No need to peel them.)
> 2 tablespoons olive oil
> 1 teaspoon Italian seasoning
> Coarse salt, such as kosher or sea salt, and freshly ground black pepper, to taste
> ¼ cup cheddar cheese, grated

1. Preheat oven to 375°F.
2. Coat a cookie sheet with cooking spray or a thin layer of oil.
3. Scrub the potatoes and cut into ¼-inch slices.
4. Toss the potatoes with the olive oil, Italian seasoning, salt and pepper.
5. Spread the potatoes on the cookie sheet. Bake until the potato slices are tender and golden brown, about 20–30 minutes.
6. Sprinkle with the cheese and place under the broiler until cheese is melted, about 5 minutes.

BROILED TOMATOES

These can be prepared ahead of time and cooked 30 minutes before dinner is served.

½ cup sour cream
½ teaspoon dried thyme
2 tablespoons bread crumbs
¼ teaspoon salt
⅛ teaspoon freshly ground black pepper
2 large tomatoes
¼ cup Parmesan cheese, grated

1. Mix the sour cream, thyme, bread crumbs, salt and pepper.

2. Remove the cores at the top of the tomatoes. Cut the tomatoes in half horizontally. Remove the seeds by pushing them out of the tomatoes with your fingers. Set the tomatoes cut side up in a greased baking dish.

3. Place 2–3 tablespoons sour cream mixture in each tomato half. Sprinkle each half with 1 tablespoon Parmesan cheese.

4. Bake at 375°F until golden brown, about 25 minutes. Place under the broiler for an additional 5 minutes to brown cheese. Watch carefully so they don't burn.

SHRIMP ARABESQUE

Get ready to lick your lips and sop up every drop of the wonderful sauce at the bottom of the pan.

- 1 pound large shrimp, shells on
- ½ stick butter, cut into thin slices
- 1 teaspoon freshly ground pepper, or to taste (We like these with plenty of pepper.)
- 2 cloves garlic, pressed

1. Preheat oven to 350°F. Lightly grease a baking dish.

2. Rinse and dry the shrimp, and spread on prepared baking dish. Spread the butter over the shrimp. Sprinkle the shrimp with the ground pepper and garlic. Bake, turning several times to coat the shrimp with butter mixture, until shrimp are opaque and cooked through, about 15–20 minutes.

3. To serve, bring out the baking dish with a loaf of French or Italian bread. Peel the shrimp with your fingers and sop up the melted butter with the bread.

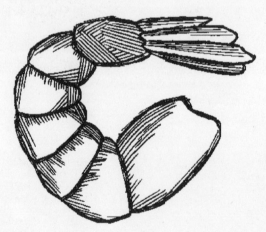

EPILOGUE

Food Noir

*T*he night is hot and black as ink. Rain curls down a dirt-streaked window framing the cruel night. The Moon, a great gray disk of ambiguity, sits in a moist fold of clouds. Drenching the night in grayish glare, she spices her wet and stormy domain with cracks of lighting and bowls of thunder.

You can't sleep. Too much champagne? Too much lovemaking? Or just too much, too much? It's midnight, stomachs growl, libidos howl for something in the dark.

You descend the stairs hand in hand, keeping the magic alive for another minute, hour or moment. On goes the squakbox. Letterman's gone, but Bogey and Bacall are there trading quips and glances of lust.

You look into each other's eyes, words are meaningless. You know what you have to do. It's time to strap on your gat, head to the kitchen and fill up that hole just below your hearts.

RICK:
You look hungry, babe. I like it when you look that way.
VERONICA:
Don't play cool with me, Rick. You like me every way.
RICK:
Never give a guy a break, huh?
VERONICA:
I've broken a few in my time, but I like you so I'll play nice.
RICK:
You call the last four hours playing nice?
VERONICA:
What do you call it?
RICK:
I see your point.
VERONICA:
How much longer we gonna stand here flappin' our gums?
RICK:
I don't get you.
VERONICA:
The word around town is that you've got a spatula that even Mother Teresa couldn't resist.

RICK:

 She's a vegan and doesn't like garlic. Some dames never learn.

VERONICA:

Don't crack wise with me, mister. Like you said, I'm hungry. And when I'm hungry, I get what I want.

RICK:

 So, what do you want baby?

VERONICA:

What every dame in this God-forsaken town wants, your eggs.

From under her full length, red silk robe, Veronica pulls out a very small, very nasty, very deadly steel-plated .22 caliber Colt automatic. It sits easily in a hand that is no stranger to cold, hard steel.

RICK:

You mean Omelette Noir.

VERONICA:

I mean eggs, now.

RICK:

Easy baby. Lead don't go in eggs. Makes 'em taste too sweet. Besides, if you plug the cook you gotta do your own dishes.

VERONICA:

Don't play me for a rube, tough guy. I've come an awful long way to taste your eggs so get cookin'. And make 'em good.

RICK:

You came all this way just for my eggs?

VERONICA:

And the appetizers.

RICK:

A dame like you can have any guy you want. Why me?

VERONICA:

Every dame wants a good man who can cook. When you find one, you grab him. You're mine now. Turn up the heat and start cookin' sweet stuff. And don't skimp. Tell me your every move. I don't trust you.

RICK:

I'm gonna cook up some home fries, and then I'll start the eggs. First, I'll scrub 3 medium potatoes, and boil them in salted water until they're half cooked, about 15 minutes. You can entertain yourself while we wait.

VERONICA:
Don't worry about me. And leave the skins on. I need my iron.
RICK:
When the potatoes are done boiling, I'll chop them into ¼-inch thick pieces and fry them in 2 tablespoons butter in a heavy fry pan over medium-low heat with a ¼ cup chopped onion, and salt and pepper to taste. Here, stir 'em around every once and a while until they're brown and crispy for me. It should take about 10 minutes. I'll start the eggs.
VERONICA:
Hey, you're good with you're hands big guy. You can fix the eggs and the potatoes at the same time. I'll watch. I like to watch.
RICK:
Okay, but while you're watching, watch that gun. You'll curdle the eggs. I'm gonna chop a green pepper and slice 2 onions. Stand back baby, the onions will make you cry.
VERONICA:
Nothing makes me cry.
RICK:
Time to melt 1 tablespoon butter in a medium skillet over a low flame and sauté the vegetables. I'll use about 1 cup of broccoli, but you can put in anything you like. Asparagus, cauliflower, green beans, whatever. Hey kid, why don't you grate that block of cheese, about ½ a cup will do. I'll crack 5 eggs into a bowl and beat them with a little salt, pepper and a couple tablespoons milk.
VERONICA:
What do you take me for? I ain't the prep cook here.
RICK:
Okay, I'll grate the cheese and add it to the eggs along with a couple slices chopped boiled ham.
VERONICA:
What happens if I want sausage?
RICK:
Then throw it in. That's the beauty of this recipe, you can add anything you want. Besides, you've got the gun so you get to call the shots.
VERONICA:
Just remember funny man that dead men don't laugh.

RICK:
You always talk like this? Anyway, now I'm gonna pour in the eggs and stir them around with a fork until they're thick and set just the way you like 'em. Why don't you set the table and pour us something to drink.
VERONICA:
How 'bout I just butter the toast?

Time lapse dissolve to 30 minutes later, same set. Rick and Veronica are sitting at the kitchen table. Empty plates dot the formica desert between them.

VERONICA:
Um....That was great. How did you learn to cook like that?
RICK:
From a book: *Food As Foreplay,* by that Cooking Couple couple.
VERONICA:
Well, it certainly tastes like you did your homework.
RICK:
Think you can put that gun away now?
VERONICA:
I kinda like being able to make you do whatever I want.
RICK:
You don't need a gun for that. All you gotta do is whistle. You know how to do that, don't cha?
VERONICA:
Yeah. Just put my lips together and blow.
RICK:
I think this is the beginning of a beautiful relationship.

Rick slides over and puts his arms around Veronica. Their lips meet as the black night turns into gray, orange and finally day. The Colt slips from her hand and drops to the floor. Rick picks up his spatula as he sweeps Veronica off her feet and up the stairs to…Champagne Saturday.

Good food, good love, good lust and good night, dear reader.

To be continued.

INDEX

Would you like to be on The Cooking Couple's special mailing list? You will receive recipe updates, discounts on future books, products and more. Just send your name, address and telephone number to:

The Cooking Couple
c/o Alexandria Press
Post Office Box 987
Cambridge, Massachusetts 02140

Would you like to see your personal romantic recipe in The Cooking Couple's next book? Ellen and Michael would love to hear from you. Send recipes to:

The Cooking Couple
c/o Alexandria Press
Post Office Box 987
Cambridge, Massachusetts 02140